D1528055

The Canadian Citizenship Test

Study Guide with 500+ Official Style
Practice Questions & Answers

*WRITTEN & PUBLISHED BY TORONTO
PUBLICATIONS*

Print ISBN: 979-8367397918
Also available in Kindle & Audiobook format

2nd Edition – Revised & Updated

Disclaimer & Copyright

Table of Contents

Introduction...5

Rights & Responsibilities (20 Questions)..................8

Who We Are (40 Questions).....................................13

Canada's History (80 Questions)............................23

Modern Canada (30 Questions)...............................42

How Canadians Govern Themselves (30 Questions)...50

Federal Elections (30 Questions)............................57

The Justice System (15 Questions).........................64

Canadian Symbols (40 Questions)...........................68

Canada's Economy (16 Questions)..........................78

Canada's Regions (105 Questions).........................82

True or False Questions...106

Rights & Responsibilities (Answers)......................117

Who We Are (Answers)..124

Canada's History (Answers)..................................136

Modern Canada (Answers).....................................160

How Canadians Govern Themselves (Answers)...169

Federal Elections (Answers)..................................178

The Justice System (Answers)...............................187

Canadian Symbols (Answers).................................192

Canada's Economy (Answers)................................204

Canada's Regions (Answers)..................................209

True or False Answers..238

BONUS: The Oath of Citizenship...........................257

Conclusion..258

Introduction

Welcome to this Canadian Citizenship Test Book. With this book, we endeavor to give you the best possible chance of passing the test, and obtaining your passport and citizenship. We've handwritten 500 questions (and answers) based off the Official Discover Canada Guide, so you can be sure these questions are unique and you won't have seen them anywhere else.

They're written in the same format that you'll get on the day of the test - multiple choice questions with 4 possible answers - so you can prepare in the most effective way possible. True or False questions are also part of the test, and you can practice these in the final chapter of this book. On the day of the test, you'll have 30 minutes to get 15 out of 20 questions correct. The test is usually written, but occasionally takes place as an interview instead. The two main things being tested are your knowledge of English (or French) and your knowledge of Canada as well as the responsibilities of being a Canadian citizen.

Here are the things you should bring to your test:
1. The notice to appear (letter inviting you to take the test)
2. Your PR (Permanent Resident) card
3. Two forms of ID, with at least one having your photograph/signature
4. Any passports or documents you included in your application

5. Any certificates that prove your ability to speak English or French
6. Any other items mentioned in the "Notice to Appear" letter

The test costs are included in the Citizenship application fee, which is around $630 for a typical application.

Anyone under 18 or anyone over 55 does not need to write the citizenship test. Please visit the https://www.canada.ca/ website for further information.

After the test, if you are successful, you will be invited to an interview. At the interview, you will get your test scores, have your documents verified, and your language skills will be on show. As long as you have passed the test and meet the other requirements, you will either receive a date for the Citizenship Ceremony, or will receive an email or letter shortly after.

The letter or email will tell you when and where your citizenship ceremony will take place. At the citizenship ceremony, there are three main events. These are: taking the oath of citizenship, signing the oath form, and receiving your Canadian Citizenship Certificate. You can bring friends and family members to the citizenship ceremony to celebrate your accomplishment. Family members' applications are processed at the same time, and if you want to attend the ceremony together, this is possible with prior arrangement.

Should you need to retake the exam (because you scored less than 15 out of 20), you can. This will usually be 4 to 10 weeks after the one you failed. If you fail twice, you will need to have a meeting with a citizenship official, where they will assess your language skills and knowledge of Canada. After a third failure, you would need to re-apply for Citizenship.

With that, let's get to the practice questions - the first chapter is "Rights & Responsibilities."

Rights & Responsibilities
(20 Questions)

1) Which year was the Magna Carta signed and introduced?

A - 1786

B - 1315

C - 1215

D - 1777

2) Which of these is not part of the Magna Carta?

A - Freedom of Conscience & Religion

B - Freedom of Speech

C - Freedom of Eating

D - Freedom of Association

3) When was the constitution of Canada amended?

A - 1982

B - 1992

C - 2002

D - 2022

4) What do you call the Right where the English and the French have equal status in the Parliament and the government?

A - Information Rights

B - Multiculturalism

C - Official Language Rights

D - Aboriginal Peoples' Rights

5) **What do you call a person's right to challenge unlawful detention by the state?**
A - Canadian Charter Rights
B - Habeas Corpus
C - Magna Carta
D - Habeas Corpus

6) **What do you call the Right where Canadians can live and work freely anywhere in Canada, apply for a passport, and leave the country freely?**
A - Aboriginal Peoples' Rights
B - Mobility Rights
C - Magna Carta
D - Official Language Rights and Minority Language Educational Rights

7) **Where was the constitution amended and proclaimed?**
A - Tokyo
B - Ottawa
C - Vancouver
D - Toronto

8) **Complete the sentence, "Whereas Canada is founded upon _____ that recognize the supremacy of God, as well as the rule of _____."**
A - Principles, Law
B - Principal, Order
C - Truth, Law
D - Truth, Order

9) What do you call the Right in which Canadians celebrate the gift of each other's presence, respect pluralism, and live in harmony?

A - Aboriginal Peoples' Rights

B - Mobility Rights

C - Habeas Corpus

D - Multiculturalism

10) Which of these best describe Aboriginal Peoples' Rights?

A - They have no rights

B - Their rights and freedoms should be respected

C - They have more rights than the French

D - They have more rights than everyone

11) Which of the following acts does Canadian criminal law not tolerate?

A - Gender-based Violence

B - Spousal Abuse

C - Forced Marriage

D - All of the above

12) Which of the following is a responsibility of a citizen?

A - Serving on a jury

B - Obeying the law

C - Voting

D - All of the above

13) No person/group is above the law. What is this responsibility called?

A - Serving on a jury

B - Habeas Corpus

C - Obeying the law

D - Protecting and enjoying the heritage

14) Is joining the military required in Canada?

A - Yes

B - No

C - Yes, but with exemptions

D - Depends on the situation

15) What do you call the citizenship responsibility where you are required to vote in federal, provincial, and local elections?

A - Voting

B - Multiculturalism

C - Serving on a jury

D - Obeying the law

16) A citizenship responsibility in which you shall respect and protect Canada's cultural, natural, and architectural heritage is called what?

A - Multiculturalism

B - Helping others in the community

C - Obeying the law

D - Protecting and enjoying our heritage and environment

17) Why is it important to serve on a jury as part of citizenship responsibility?

A - It avoids waste and pollution

B - It is easy

C - It's a privilege as the justice system relies on the impartial and unbiased jurors for it to work

D - It doesn't last long

18) Which of the following can you join as a way to serve and contribute to Canada?

A - Navy

B - Army

C - Air Force

D - All of the above

19) What can you learn when you join the Canadian Forces?

A - Discipline

B - Responsibility

C - Skills

D - All of the Above

20) What do you call the citizenship responsibility in which you help other people in your community by volunteering?

A - Obeying the law

B - Helping others in the community

C - Protecting the heritage

D - Taking responsibility for oneself and one's family

Who We Are (40 Questions)

1) Who are the founding people of Canada?
A - French
B - Aboriginal
C - British
D - All of the above

2) What is Canada known as around the world?
A - Strong and Independent Country
B - Strong and Free Country
C - Independent and Free Country
D - None of the above

3) Canada is the only country with what kind of government in North America?
A - Constitutional monarchy
B - Federalism
C - Democracy
D - Dictatorship

4) The institution upholds a commitment to which of the following?
A - Peace
B - Order
C - Good Government
D – All of the above

5) What did poets and songwriters hail Canada as?

A - Great Denomination

B - Grand Dominion

C - Great Dominion

D - Grand Denomination

6) What do you call the 1867 constitutional document in which Peace, Order, and Good Government was used as a key phrase?

A - Magna Carta

B - Royal Proclamation

C - Canadian Charter of Rights and Freedom

D - British North America Act

7) Where were the ancestors of the Aboriginal people believed to have migrated from?

A - Europe

B - Asia

C - France

D - America

8) From what period in time did the government place aboriginal children in residential schools to help educate them?

A - 1800s until 2000s

B - 1800s until 1980s

C - 1970s until 1980s

D - 1700s until 1800s

9) Who was the monarch that signed the Royal Proclamation of 1763?

A - King George III
B - King George IV
C - Queen Victoria
D - Queen Elizabeth

10) What do you call the right that was guaranteed through the Royal Proclamation of 1763?
A - Magna Carta
B - Great Charter of Freedom
C - Territorial Rights
D - Canadian Charter of Rights and Freedom

11) What does the term *Aboriginal people* refer to in today's world?
A - Indian, Inuit, and Mètis
B - Indian, Irish, and Mètis
C - English, Inuit, and Mètis
D - None of the above

12) Which of these were mostly prohibited in the residential schools that the federal government established during the 1800s-1980s?
A - French languages
B - English languages
C - Aboriginal languages and cultural practices
D - None of the above

13) In what year did Ottawa formally apologize to the former students who were abused?
A - 2005

B - 2006

C - 2007

D - 2008

14) When did the term "First Nations" begin to be used?

A - 1700s

B - 1890s

C - 1950s

D - 1970s

15) Who was the 1st Baron Tweedsmuir as well as the popular Governor General of Canada from 1935 to 1940?

A - John Buchon

B - Eric Buchan

C - Eric Buchon

D - John Buchan

16) What do you call the Aboriginal people who live in small scattered communities in the Arctic?

A - Inuit

B - Mètis

C - Indian

D - Icelander

17) Where do the majority of Mètis people live?

A - Central Canada

B - Prairie Provinces

C - North Territories

D - None of the above

18) What do you call the dialect that the Mètis people speak?

A - Inuktitut

B - Michif

C - Mètisians

D - Aboriginal

19) What does Inuit mean in the Inuktitut language?

A - The friends

B - The people

C - The country

D - The community

20) The Mètis are the descendants of what mixed ancestry?

A - Aboriginal and European

B - European and Indian

C - Irish and Indian

D - Indian and Aboriginal

21) What are the official languages of Canada?

A - English and Chinese

B - French and Irish

C - English and French

D - French and Chinese

22) What do you call people who use English as their first language?

A - Francophones

B - Anglophones

C - Bilinguals

D - None of the above

23) What do you call people who use French as their first language?

A - Anglophones

B - English

C - Bilingual

D - Francophones

24) What is the only official province which is bilingual?

A - Ottawa

B - Toronto

C - New Brunswick

D - Vancouver

25) What do you call the event that happened during the 1700s where most Acadians were deported from their homeland?

A - Great Upheaval

B - Great Uproar

C - Grand Upheaval

D - Grand Uproar

26) When did the House of Commons recognize the Quebecois as a formed nation within a united Canada?

A - 2010

B - 2006

C - 1900

D - 2000

27) What do Anglophones generally refer to themselves as?

A - English Aboriginal

B - Aboriginal Canadian

C - French Canadian

D - English Canadian

28) Who established the basic way of life in the English-speaking area?

A - English, Welsh, Scottish, and Irish settlers

B - English, Welsh, Indian, and Irish settlers

C - French, Welsh, Scottish, and Irish settlers

D - None of the Above

29) What did you call people of Quebec?

A - Quebec

B - Inuit

C - Quebecers

D - English

30) What is the estimated count of English and French speakers as of today?

A - 20 million Anglophones, 8 million Francophones

B - 18 million Anglophones, 8 million Francophones

C - 20 million Anglophones, 7 million Francophones

D - 18 million Anglophones, 7 million Francophones

31) What is Canada often referred to as?

A - Land of Settlers

B - Land of Immigrants

C - State of Immigrants

D - State of Settlers

32) What is the second most-spoken language in Vancouver and Toronto?

A - Indian language

B - French language

C - Korean language

D - Chinese language

33) What is the largest religious affiliation in Canada?

A - Catholic

B - Protestant

C - Muslim

D - Jews

34) Why did Canada partner with faith communities?

A - To help promote social welfare

B - To help provide schools and healthcare

C - To help resettle refugees

D - All of the above

35) Which of the following is also included in Canada's diversity?

A - Young and old Canadians

B - Gay and lesbian Canadians

C - Immigrants and soldiers

D - None of the above

36) What is the estimated percentage of the population that speaks Chinese at home in Vancouver?

A - 43% of the population

B - 15% of the population

C - 13% of the population

D - 33% of the population

37) What is the estimated percentage of the population that speaks Chinese at home in Toronto?

A - 7% of the population

B - 17% of the population

C - 0.7% of the population

D - 27% of the population

38) Who is the Olympian that is a descendant of Black Loyalists, escaped slaves and freed men and women of American origin - who in the 1970s fled to Canada from America?

A - Abigail Strait

B - Marjorie Turner-Bailey

C - Vasek Pospisil

D - Piper Gilles

39) In the 1970s, most immigrants came from what countries?

A - Australia

B - European

C - Asian

D - America

40) New Canadians are expected to embrace democratic principles such as what?
A - Rule of community
B - Rule of land
C - Rule of monarchy
D - Rule of law

Canada's History (80 Questions)

1) Who were the natives occupying the region that the Europeans found when they explored Canada?

A - Asians

B - Indians

C - Irish

D - Americans

2) Why were the natives called Indians?

A - Because the Europeans saw their clothing style

B - Because the Europeans thought they had reached the North Indies

C - Because the Europeans noticed the different settlement

D - Because the Europeans thought they had reached the East Indies

3) What do you call the native people of the Great Lakes region?

A - Inuit

B - Aboriginal

C - Huron-Wendat

D - Nomads

4) What were the native people of the Northwest, Cree and Dene?

A - Hunter-gatherers

B - Fishermen

C - Farmers

D - Software Developers

5) How do West Coast natives preserve fish?

A - By deboning

B - By drying and smoking

C - By using salt

D - By preserving in a jar

6) What is common among aboriginal groups as they compete for land, resources, and prestige?

A - Trading

B - Business

C - Farming

D - Warfare

7) Why did a large number of aboriginal people die of European diseases?

A - Because they lacked immunity

B - Because of huge volume of settlers

C - Because of poor hygiene

D - None of the above

8) What did the Aboriginals and Europeans form that laid the foundation of Canada?

A - Economic Bonds

B - Religious Bonds

C - Military Bonds

D - All of the above

9) **Who was the first person to map out Canada's East Coast?**
   A - Peter Cabot
   B - John Cabot
   C - Peter John
   D - John Shore

10) **Who was the first European to explore St. Lawrence River and discover present-day Quebec City and Montreal?**
   A - Jacques Cabot
   B - Henry Cartier
   C - Henry Cabot
   D - Jacques Cartier

11) **Where did the Vikings who colonized Greenland come from?**
   A - Ireland
   B - Iceland
   C - The Arctic
   D - Canada

12) **What do you call the remains of the settlement of Vikings who colonized Greenland, which is a World Heritage site today?**
   A - l'Anse aux Meadows
   B - The Ships
   C - The Lost Town
   D - The Eiffel Tower

13) When did European exploration begin?
   A - 1500
   B - 1978
   C - 1497
   D - 1450

14) How many voyages did Jacques Cartier make between 1534 and 1542?
   A - Two
   B - Three
   C - Four
   D - Five

15) What does the Iroquoian word Kanata mean?
   A - People
   B - Settlers
   C - Community
   D - Village

16) When did the word Canada begin appearing on maps?
   A - 1600s
   B - 1670s
   C - 1550s
   D - 1480s

17) Who refused to surrender Quebec to England in 1690?
   A - Count Pierre
   B - Count Frontenac
   C - Sir Guy Carleton
   D - Lord Dochester

18) Who was the Governor of Quebec who defended the rights of Canadians?

A - Count Frontenac

B - Henry Cabot

C - Jacques Cartier

D - Sir Guy Carleton

19) In what year did Sir Guy Carleton defeat an American military invasion of Quebec?

A - 1775

B - 1780

C - 1890

D - 1875

20) Who were the French explorers who established the first European settlement north of Florida?

A - Pierre de Monts and Samuel de Champlain

B - Pierre de Champlain and Samuel de Monts

C - Pierre de Cartier and Samuel de Monts

D - Pierre de Champlain and Samuel de Champlain

21) What did they call Nova Scotia before?

A - Arctic

B - Metis

C - Acadia

D - Kanata

22) When did the French and Iroquois make peace?

A - 1600

B - 1701

C - 1700

D - 1601

23) What drove the vast fur-trade economy of the French and Aboriginal people?

A - Demand for beaver pelts

B - Demand for squirrel pelts

C - Demand for fox furs

D - Demand for bear furs

24) Who gave the Hudson's Bay Company exclusive rights over watershed draining in Hudson Bay?

A - Jacques Cartier

B - John Cabolt

C - King Charles II of England

D - Queen Elizabeth II

25) When was the trading right over watershed draining granted?

A - 1760

B - 1860

C - 1870

D - 1670

26) When did the English colonies along the Atlantic seaboard become richer and more populous than New France?

A - The early 1700s

B - The early 1800s

C - The early 1600s

D - The early 1500s

27) What did they call the skilled and courageous men who traveled by canoe and formed a strong alliance with the First Nations?

A - Voyageurs and coureurs des bois

B - Paddlers and boaters

C - Settlers and immigrants

D - None of the above

28) In what battle did the British defeat the French at Quebec City during the year of 1759?

A - Battle of the Plains of Canada

B - Battle of the Plains of Quebec

C - Battle of the Plains of Abraham

D - Battle of the British and French

29) What did Great Britain rename the colony after the war?

A - Province of Britain

B - Canada

C - Kanata

D - Province of Quebec

30) What did the British Parliament pass to help better govern the French Roman Catholic majority?

A - Quebec Act of 1784

B - Quebec Act of 1774

C - Quebec Act of 1874

D - Quebec Act of 1884

31) What was formed after the 13 British colonies south of Quebec declared independence?

A - United States

B - Canada

C - Ireland

D - Asia

32) When did the 13 colonies declare independence?

A - 1876

B - 1796

C - 1786

D - 1776

33) What did they call people who were loyal to the crown - who fled the oppression during the American Revolution, and settled in Nova Scotia and Quebec?

A - Settlers

B - Aboriginals

C - Loyalists

D - Villagers

34) Who led thousands of Loyalist Mohawk Indians into Canada?

A - Joseph Cartier

B - Joseph Brant

C - John Brant

D - John Cartier

35) Where was the first representative assembly elected?

A - Halifax, Nova Scotia in 1768

B - Toronto in 1758

C - Ottawa in 1558

D - Halifax, Nova Scotia in 1758

36) What divided Quebec into Upper Canada and Lower Canada?

A - The Constitutional Act of 1781

B - The Constitutional Act of 1771

C - The Constitutional Act of 1791

D - None of the above

37) Who was the first Lieutenant Governor of Upper Canada and founder of the City of York?

A - Lieutenant-Colonel John Graves Simcoe

B - Jacques Cartier

C - Count Frontenac

D - John Brant

38) What was the weekly newspaper that was dedicated to anti-slavery, black immigration to Canada, temperance, and upholding British rule?

A - The Canadian Newspaper

B - The Provincial Newspaper

C - The Canadian Freeman

D - The Provincial Freeman

39) When did the British Parliament abolish the buying and selling of slaves throughout the empire?

A - 1633

B - 1733

C - 1833

D - 1933

40) In what year did some black Nova Scotians move on to establish Freetown, Sierra Leone (West Africa)?

A - 1878

B - 1777

C - 1792

D - 1972

41) What trade did the first companies of Canada compete in?

A - Mining

B - Fur trade

C - Fishing

D - Logging

42) Who ruled the waves after the defeat of Napoleon Bonaparte in the Battle of Trafalgar?

A - The Royal Navy

B - The Americans

C - The Indians

D - The Royal Marine

43) When was the Battle of Trafalgar?

    A - 1905

    B - 1925

    C - 1805

    D - 1825

44) When did the United States launch an invasion to conquer Canada?

    A - June 1912

    B - June 1812

    C - July 1812

    D - July 1812

45) Who was the Major-General who captured Detroit but was killed at Queenston Heights while defending against an American attack?

    A - Lieutenant-Colonel Charles de Salaberry

    B - Chief Tecumseh

    C - Major-General Sir Isaac Breck

    D - Major-General Sir Isaac Brock

46) Who was the person who walked 30km to warn James FitzGibbon of an American attack?

    A - Laura Secord

    B - Duke of Wellington

    C - Lana Secord

    D - Agnes Macphail

47) **When did Upper and Lower Canada unite as the Province of Canada?**
    A - 1940
    B - 1740
    C - 1840
    D - 1640

48) **Who was the champion of French language rights that became the first head of a responsible government in Canada in 1849?**
    A - Sir John Alexander Macdonald
    B - Sir George-Étienne Cartier
    C - Sir Louis-Hippolyte La Fontaine
    D - Louis Riel

49) **What was the British North American colony who first attained full responsible government?**
    A - Nova Scotia
    B - Ottawa
    C - Quebec
    D - Hudson Bay

50) **What do you call the representatives who worked together to establish a new country?**
    A - Fathers of Communication
    B - Fathers of Congregation
    C - Fathers of Configuration
    D - Fathers of Confederation

51) What are the two levels of government?

    A - Federal and Provocational

    B - Upper and Lower Canada

    C - Federal and Provincial

    D - Territorial and Provincial

52) What do you call the celebration that is held every July 1st, also known as Dominion Day?

    A - Manitoba Day

    B - Sir John A. Macdonald Day

    C - Canada Day

    D - Quebec Day

53) Who suggested the term Dominion of Canada in 1864?

    A - Sir Leonard Macdonald

    B - Sir Leonard Tilley

    C - Lord Durham

    D - Sir Gregory Tilley

54) What inspired the term Dominion of Canada?

    A - A song

    B - A poem

    C - Psalm 72 in the Bible

    D - A quote

55) Who was Canada's first Prime Minister?

    A - Sir John Alexander Macdonald

    B - Major-General Sir Isaac Brock

    C - Sir Louis-Hippolyte La Fontaine

    D - Sir George-Étienne Cartier

56) Where was the first Prime Minister of Canada born?

A - Scotland

B - Ireland

C - Greenland

D - Iceland

57) Where can you find the portrait of Sir John A. Macdonald?

A - $5 bill

B - $1 bill

C - $10 bill

D - $20 bill

58) In what year did some believe that the British West Indies should become part of Canada?

A - 1870s

B - 1920s

C - 1990s

D - 1780s

59) What did the first elected Assembly of Lower Canada debate on January 21, 1793?

A - Who to elect as Prime Minister

B - Whether to use both French and English

C - Whether to let women vote

D - Whether to free the slaves

60) Who seized Fort Garry from Hudson's Bay Company in 1869?

A - Prime Minister Macdonald

B - Louis Riel

C - Sir Louis-Hippolyte La Fontaine

D - Lord Durham

61) In what year did Ottawa send soldiers to retake Fort Garry?

A - 1870

B - 1990

C - 1889

D - 1875

62) In what year did Prime Minister Macdonald establish the North West Mounted Police (NWMP)?

A - 1983

B - 1883

C - 1973

D - 1873

63) Who assigned Canada's national colors white and red in 1921?

A - King George II

B - King George V

C - Queen Elizabeth II

D - Lord Durham

64) Who became the first French-Canadian Prime Minister since the Confederation and encouraged immigration to the West?

A - Sir George-Étienne Cartier

B - Sir Louis-Hippolyte La Fontaine

C - Sir John Alexander Macdonald

D - Sir Wilfrid Laurier

65) What is the other term for the South African War that happened during 1899-1902?

A - Boer War

B - South War

C - Canada War

D - World War

66) What did they call the nurses that served in the Royal Canadian Army Medical Corps?

A - Ladybirds

B - Blue Nurses

C - Lady Nurses

D - Bluebirds

67) What do you call the effort by women to achieve the rights to vote?

A - Women's Voting Movement

B - Women's Suffrage Movement

C - Women's Rights Confederation

D - None of the above

68) Who was the first woman to serve as a Member of Parliament in 1921?

A - Laura Riel

B - Dr. Emily Stowe

C - Agnes Macphail

D - Denys Arcand

69) What do you call the free association of states that the British Empire evolved into after the First World War?

A - Britain Commonwealth of Nations

B - British Commonwealth of People

C - British Commonwealth of Nations

D - Britain Commonwealth of People

70) What poem did Lieutenant-Colonel John McCrae compose in 1915 that is often recited on Remembrance Day?

A - In Flanders Fields

B - In Flowers Fields

C - In Flanders Garden

D - In Flowers Garden

71) What led to the Great Depression or the "Dirty Thirties"?

A - Rebellion

B - Riot

C - World War II

D - Stock Market Crash

72) In what years was the Bank of Canada created?

A - 1844

B - 1934

C - 1794

D - 1994

73) What do you call the invasion of Normandy in Northern France where Canadian troops took Juno Beach from the German Army?

A - D-Day

B - Completion Day

C - Canadian Invasion

D - None of the above

74) In what year did the Second World War begin?

A - 1949

B - 1839

C - 1939

D - 1849

75) Who took part in the Battle of Britain for Canada?

A - Royal Canadian Navy

B - Royal Canadian Air Force

C - Marines

D - Volunteers

76) Who protected the convoys of ships against German submarines during the Battle of the Atlantic?

A - Royal Canadian Navy

B - Royal Canadian Air Force

C - Marines

D - Volunteers

THE CANADIAN CITIZENSHIP TEST

77) **When did Japan surrender and the end four years of war in the Pacific?**
   A - August 24, 1975
   B - August 14, 1965
   C - August 24, 1955
   D - August 14, 1945

78) **What led to the relocation of Canadians of Japanese origin - and the sale of their property without compensation?**
   A - State of war and public opinion
   B - Stock market crash
   C - Rebellion
   D - None of the above

79) **What do you call the Royal Navy frigate which led the captured USS Chesapeake into Halifax harbor?**
   A - HMS Charlotte
   B - HMS Shannon
   C - HMS Sharon
   D - HMS Michael

80) **In what year was the captured USS Chesapeake led into the Halifax Harbour?**
   A - 1813
   B - 1887
   C - 1897
   D - 1883

Modern Canada (30 Questions)

1) **What was discovered in Alberta in 1947 that began Canada's modern energy industry?**
   A - Oil
   B - Electricity
   C - Turbines
   D - Gold

2) **What is the meaning of the acronym GATT?**
   A - General Agreement on Taxes and Trades
   B - General Agreement on Terrain and Trades
   C - General Agreement on Tariffs and Trades
   D - None of the above

3) **In what year were the majority of Canadians able to afford adequate food and clothing for the first time?**
   A - 1996
   B - 1967
   C - 1926
   D - 1951

4) **What do you call the social assistance program that ensures common elements and a basic standard coverage?**
   A - Canada Health Act
   B - Healthy People Act
   C - Canada Welfare Act
   D - Canada Insurance Act

5) **When was Employment Insurance introduced by the federal government?**
   A - 1840
   B - 1770
   C - 1940
   D - 1970

6) **In what year was Old Age Security devised?**
   A - 1922
   B - 1950
   C - 1976
   D - 1927

7) **Who provides publicly funded education?**
   A - Parliament members
   B - Provinces and territories
   C - Volunteers
   D - Churches

8) **What did they call the era of rapid change that Quebec experienced in the 1960s?**
   A - Quiet Retaliation
   B - Quiet Revolution
   C - Quebec Revolution
   D - Quebec Retaliation

9) **In what year did the Parliament establish the Royal Commission on Bilingualism and Biculturalism?**
   A - 1925
   B - 1976

C - 1963

D - 1988

10) This act guarantees French as well as English services by the federal government.

A - Official Languages Act (1969)

B - Official Languages Act (1869)

C - Roaring Twenties Act (1869)

D - Official Tenties Act (1969)

11) What is the international association of French-speaking countries that Canada helped found?

A - La Anglophonie

B - French-English Association

C - French Language Association

D - La Francophonie

12) In what year was the La Francophonie founded?

A - 1960

B - 1970

C - 1980

D - 1990

13) Who were the last to gain the right to vote in 1948?

A - Japanese-English

B - Japanese-Canadians

C - British-Canadian

D - Japanese-British

44

14) In what year did the Communist victory in the Vietnam war lead to many Vietnamese fleeing and searching for refuge in Canada?

A - 1975

B - 1985

C - 1889

D - 1995

15) What was founded in 1920 when a style of painting captured the rugged wilderness?

A - Team of Seven

B - Group with Seven

C - Team with Seven

D - Group of Seven

16) Who pioneered modern Inuit art with etchings, prints, and soapstone sculptures?

A - Denys Arcand

B - Louis-Philippe Hébert

C - Norman Jewison

D - Atom Egoyan

17) What sport did the Canadian James Naismith invent in 1891?

A - Basketball

B - Tennis

C - Hockey

D - Football

18) Who became the world record sprinter and double Olympic gold medalist in 1996 at the Olympic Summer Games?

A - Denys Arcand

B - Wayne Gretzky

C - Marshall McLuhan

D - Donovan Bailey

19) What did they call the cross-country run that Terry Fox started in 1980 to raise money for cancer research?

A - Marathon of Faith

B - Marathon of Hope

C - Run of Hope

D - Run of Faith

20) In what year did the British Columbian Rick Hansen circle the globe to raise funds for spinal cord research?

A - 1985

B - 1885

C - 1785

D - 1685

21) What did Sir Frederick Banting and Charles Best discover to treat diabetes?

A - Antibiotic

B - Penicillin

C - Booster

D - Insulin

22) In what year did Paul Henderson score the important goal for Canada in the Canada-Soviet Summit Series, often referred to as "the goal heard around the world"?

A - 1872

B - 1772

C - 1972

D - 1982

23) What does the acronym NATO stand for?

A - North Atlantic Team Organization

B - North Atlantic Treaty Organization

C - North Arctic Treaty Organization

D - North Acadia Treaty Organization

24) Who is the Olympic gold medalist and prominent activist for gay and lesbian Canadians?

A - Edmonton Oilers

B - Chantal Peticlerc

C - Mark Tewksbury

D - Rick Hansen

25) In which team did Wayne Gretzky play from 1978-1988?

A - Edmonton Oilers

B - Boston Bruins

C - Montreal Canadiens

D - Calgary Flames

26) In what year were the Aboriginal people granted the right to vote?

A - 1660

B - 1760

C - 1860

D - 1960

27) In what year did the Canadian Space Agency and Canadian astronauts participate in space exploration, using the Canadian-designed and built Canadarm?

A - 1889

B - 1989

C - 1879

D - 1979

28) What did Joseph-Armand Bombardier invent?

A - The Snowmobile

B - The Light Bulb

C - Insulin

D - The Telephone

29) What did Matthew Evans and Henry Woodward invent?

A - Telephone

B - Electric light bulb

C - Insulin

D - Electric car

30) Who invented the first cardiac pacemaker?

A - Dr. Wilder Penfield

B - Sir Sanford Flemming

C - Jim Balsillie

D - Dr. John A. Hopps

How Canadians Govern Themselves (30 Questions)

1) How many governments are there in Canada?
A - Three
B - One
C - Four
D - Two

2) What do you call a government that takes responsibility for matters of both national and international concern?
A - Federal State
B - National State
C - Municipal
D - Judicial

3) Which of the following is not in the scope of the Federal State?
A - Foreign Policy
B - Interprovincial Trade and Communications
C - Criminal Law and Citizenship
D - None of the above

4) Which of the following is not part of the responsibility of the Provincial government?
A - Education
B - Defence
C - Health
D - Municipal Government

5) The federal government and the provinces share what jurisdiction?

A - Agriculture and Defence

B - Agriculture and Immigration

C - Education and Defence

D - Immigration and Health

6) Which of these allows provinces to form policies for their own populations?

A - State

B - Democratic

C - Federalism

D - Provincial

7) What do you call the system in which members are elected to the House of Commons in Ottawa - by the people?

A - Federalism

B - Sovereignty

C - Parliamentary Democracy

D - Federal Democracy

8) Which of the following is not part of the responsibility of the representatives?

A - Approving and monitoring expenditures

B - Keeping the government accountable

C - Passing of laws

D - None of the above

9) Who is responsible to the elected representatives?

A - Cabinet ministers

B - Sovereign

C - Prime Minister

D - Assembly members

10) The Parliament has how many parts?

A - Three

B - Four

C - Five

D - One

11) Which of the following is not part of the Parliament?

A - House of Commons

B - Senate

C - Municipal

D - Sovereign

12) Who is responsible in selecting Cabinet members as well as responsible for the operations and policy of the government?

A - President

B - Prime Minister

C - King

D - House Speaker

13) What do you call the chamber elected by the people every four years?

A - Member of the jury

B - Cabinet members

C - House of Representative

D - House of Commons

14) Who appoints the Senators on the advice of the Prime Minister?

A - The King

B - Representatives

C - The Governor General

D - Cabinet Ministers

15) Until what age can the Senators stay in position?

A - 75 years old

B - 85 years old

C - 100 years old

D - 65 years old

16) What do you call the proposal for new laws that both the House of Commons and Senate consider and review?

A - Laws

B - Legislative

C - Proposals

D - Bills

17) What does the Governor General grant on behalf of the sovereign before passing a bill to become a law?

A - Royal seal

B - Royal assent

C - Medal

D - Signature

18) How many steps are there in making a law?

A - Four

B - Five

C - Six

D - Seven

19) What is the 5th step in the legislative process of making a new law?

A - The members debate and vote on the bill

B - Members can make other amendments

C - Members debate the bill's principle

D - Committee members study the bill clause by clause

20) What happens in the 2nd step in the legislative process of making a new law?

A - Committee members study the bill clause by clause

B - The members debate the bills principle

C - The bill follows a similar process in the senate

D - Members debate and vote on the bill

21) At what age can Canadian citizens vote?

A - 16 years old

B- 17 years old

C - 19 years old

D - 18 years old

22) Who represents the sovereign in the 10 provinces?

A - Governor General

B - Prime Minister

C - Lieutenant Governor

D - Cabinet members

23) Who appoints the Lieutenant Governor on the advice of the Prime Minister?

A - Governor General

B - Lieutenant Governor

C - Prime Minister

D - King

24) Who is the 28th Governor General since the Confederation?

A - David Jonstone

B - David Jonson

C - David Hudson

D - David Johnston

25) In the three territories, who represents the federal government and plays a ceremonial role?

A - Cabinet members

B - Commissioner

C - Speaker

D - Governor General

26) Which are not members of the legislature?

A - Members of the Legislative Assembly

B - Members of the Provincial Parliament

C - Members of the National Association

D - Members of the House of Assembly

27) In each province, who has a similar role to the Prime Minister in the federal government?

A - Premier

B - Lieutenant General

C - Commissioner

D - Head of State

28) Which of the following is not included in the three branches of government?

A - Legislative

B - Judicial

C - Executive

D - Federal

29) Complete these three key facts about Canada's system of government: Canada is a federal state, a parliamentary democracy, and a _____ monarchy.

A - Constitutional

B - Provincial

C - Institutional

D - Federal

30) In what Act were the responsibilities of the federal and provincial government defined?

A - Constitution Act, 1967

B - Constitution Act, 1867

C - Constitution Act, 1987

D - Constitution Act, 1897

Federal Elections (30 Questions)

1) When is the federal election held under legislation passed by Parliament?

A - Second Monday in October, every four years

B - Third Monday in October, every four years

C - Second Monday in November, every four years

D - Third Monday in November, every four years

2) What do you call the geographical area represented by a member of Parliament (MP)?

A - Electoral District

B - Sovereign

C - Electoral Post

D - Voting District

3) Canada is divided into how many electoral districts?

A - 508

B - 448

C - 318

D - 308

4) What do you call people who run for office?

A - Members

B - Candidates

C - Solicitors

D - Officials

5) Which of the following shows that you are eligible to vote?

A - Being a Canadian Citizen

B - Being on the voter's list

C - Being at least 18 years old on voting day

D - All of the above

6) Who produces the voters' lists used during federal elections and referendums?

A - Cabinet members

B - Electors Committee

C - Elections Canada

D - None of the above

7) What do Elections Canada mail to each person whose name is found in the National Register of Electors?

A - Voter Information Card

B - Ballots

C - Lists of candidates

D - Guide in voting

8) Which Canadian law ensures that nobody can watch you vote?

A - The right to vote freely

B - The right to skip vote

C - The right to a secret ballot

D - None of the above

9) What do you call the party in power that holds over 50% of seats in the House of Commons?

A - Minority government

B - Majority government

C - Minority committee

D - Majority committee

10) What do you call the party that holds less than 50% of the seats in the House of Commons?

A - Majority committee

B - Minority committee

C - Majority government

D - Minority government

11) Who chooses the ministers of the Crown from members of the House of Commons?

A - Secretary

B - Lieutenant General

C - Governor General

D - Prime Minister

12) Who are responsible for running the federal government departments?

A - Cabinet Ministers

B - King

C - Prime Minister

D - Governor General

13) What do you call the Cabinet ministers and the Prime Minister?

A - Members

B - Parliaments

C - Cabinet

D - Commoners

14) What do you call the party that peacefully opposes or tries to improve government proposals?

A - House of Opposition

B - Opposition Parties

C - Opposition Committee

D - None of the above

15) Which of the following is not included in the current three major political parties represented in the House of Commons?

A - Conservative

B - Liberal

C - Federal

D - New Democratic

16) How many procedures are there in voting?

A - Five

B - Six

C - Seven

D - Eight

17) What should you do if you don't get a voter information card?

A - Call your local elections office

B - Skip and vote in the next election

C - Use a family's voter information card

D - None of the above

18) When voting, how do you mark the name of the candidate of your choice?

A - Shade the circle next to the candidate.

B - Put an "X" in the circle next to the candidates name.

C - Cross out the name of the candidate

D - Underline the name of the candidate

19) Who will be the one to tear off the ballot number after you have finished voting?

A - You

B - Police

C - Poll Official

D - Ballot numbers should not be teared off

20) Where do you deposit your ballot after voting?

A - At home

B - In the ballot box

C - Give it to the poll official

D - Throw it in the trash

21) What do you call laws that the Municipal government passes which only affects the local community?

A - Bill

B - By-laws

C - Laws

D - Proposals

22) What is the other term for mayor which councils usually include in the municipal government?

A - Lieutenant-Governor

B - Cabinet

C - Chief

D - Revee

23) What is the other term for councilors which councils usually include in the municipal government?

A - Eldermen

B - Aldermen

C - Chief

D - Revee

24) Which of the following is part of the responsibility of municipalities?

A - Snow removal

B - Public transit

C - Urban or regional planning

D - All of the above

25) Which of the following is not part of the responsibility of the Members of the Legislative Assembly?

A - Highways

B - Education

C - Recycling Programs

D - Property and Civil Rights

26) The following are shared responsibilities of both Members of Parliament and the Members of the Legislative Assembly, except for one, which is it?

A - Criminal Justice

B - Agriculture

C - Environment
D - Immigration

27) Who are the ones elected during the Provincial and Territorial Election?
A - Members of the House of Assembly
B - Members of the Provincial Parliament
C - Members of the National Association
D - Members of the Legislative Assembly

28) Who are the ones elected during the Federal Elections?
A - Prime Minister
B - Members of Parliament
C - Cabinet Members
D - Governor-General

29) Who are the ones elected during the Municipal Elections?
A - Mayor and Councilors
B - Mayor and Reeve
C - Councilors and Aldermen
D - None of the Above

30) Which of the following is not part of the responsibility of the Members of Parliament?
A - Aboriginal Affairs
B - National Defence
C - Social and Community Health
D - International Trade

The Justice System (15 Questions)

1) **This guarantees everyone due process under the law.**
   A - Bills
   B - Canadian Justice System
   C - Rights
   D - Judge

2) **What is meant by the term "Presumption of Innocence"?**
   A - Everyone is innocent until proven guilty
   B - Everyone is not innocent until proven guilty
   C - Everyone is guilty until proven innocent
   D - None of the above

3) **This principle states that the government must respect all legal rights each person is entitled to under the law.**
   A - Rule of Law
   B - Democratic Principles
   C - Due Process
   D - Freedom under the law

4) **What symbolizes the impartial manner of our laws - blind to all considerations but all facts?**
   A - Blindfolded Lady Justice
   B - Scale
   C - Hammer
   D - Statue of Liberty

5) **These are intended to provide order in society, and to express the values/beliefs of Canadians.**
A - Bills
B - Rights
C - Laws
D - Proposal

6) **What do you call Canada's highest court?**
A - House of Commons
B - Supreme Court of Canada
C - Trial Court
D - Federal Court of Canada

7) **Which court deals with matters concerning the federal government?**
A - House of Commons
B - Supreme Court of Canada
C - Trial Court
D - Federal Court of Canada

8) **The following courts deal with civil cases involving small sums of money. Which of the following is not accurate?**
A - Federal Court of Canada
B - Traffic Court
C - Family Court
D - Small Claims Court

9) **Who keeps the people safe and enforces the law?**
A - Councilors

B - Members of Parliament

C - Mayor

D - Police

10) What do you call the police forces that are present in Ontario and Quebec?

A - Members of the Police Force

B - Provincial Police Forces

C - Quebec Police Force

D - Ontario Police Force

11) What do you call the police force who enforces federal laws throughout Canada?

A - Royal Canadian Member Police

B - Royal Canadian Mounted Police

C - Royal Captain Member Police

D - Royal Captain Mounted Police

12) Who can help you with legal problems and act for you in court?

A - Lawyers

B - Police

C - Jury

D - Witness

13) This place has an essential role in punishing criminals and deterring crime.

A - House

B - Crime Scene

C - Prisons

D - Parliament

14) What is another term for Trial Court?

A - Court of Municipal

B - Provincial court

C - Court of Commons

D - Court of Queen's Bench

15) In what situations can you ask the police for help?

A - If there's been an accident

B - If you lost something

C - If you see a crime taking place

D - All of the above

Canadian Symbols (40 Questions)

1) What has been the symbol of Canada for 400 years? It is a symbol of government, including the parliament, the legislature, the courts, police services, and the Canadian Forces?

A - Maple leaf

B - Crown

C - Pen

D - Lady Justice

2) In what year was the new Canadian flag raised?

A - 1965

B - 1865

C - 1995

D - 1975

3) Where did the red-white-red pattern of the flag come from?

A - From the flag of the British Royal Army

B - Proposed by the House of Commons

C - From the flag of the Royal Military College

D - None of the above

4) What do you call the official Royal Flag?

A - Unified Jack

B - Union Flag

C - Unified Nation

D - Union Jack

5) **What is Canada's best-known symbol that was adopted by French Canadians in the 1700s and carved in the headstones of the fallen soldiers?**

A - Crown

B - Lady Justice

C - Maple Leaf

D - Pen

6) **What do you call the symbol that was adopted by the French king in 496? It also became a symbol of French royalty?**

A - Maple Leaf

B - Lily Flower

C - Lily of the Valley

D - Rose

7) **What is another name for Lily Flower, which was used as the symbol of French royalty?**

A - Fleur-de-lys

B - Flower of French

C - Royal Flower

D - None of the above

8) **What is the coat of arms and national motto that Canada adopted after the First World War?**

A - National Pride of Canadians

B - To you from failing hands we throw

C - We lived, felt dawn, saw sunset glow

D - A mari usque ad mare

9) **What does the coat of arms and national motto mean?**
A - From land to land
B - From land to sea
C - From sea to sea
D - From land to shining sea

10) **Which of the following is not included in the Parliament Buildings that embody the French, English, and Aboriginal traditions?**
A - Stained glass
B - Arches
C - Sculptures
D - Scale

11) **When were the parliament buildings completed?**
A -1950s
B - 1960s
C - 1970s
D - 1980s

12) **What destroyed the Centre Block in 1916?**
A - Accidental fire
B - Arson
C - Riot
D - Earthquake

13) **In what year was the Centre Block rebuilt?**
A - 1722
B - 1827
C - 1977

D - 1922

14) What was built in 1927 to remember the First World War?

A - Statue of Liberty

B - The Peace Tower

C - Parliament Buildings

D - Eiffel Tower

15) What do you call the books in the Memorial Chamber that holds soldiers, sailors, and airmen's names - of those who died serving Canada in war/on duty?

A - Obituary

B - Book of the Dead

C - Books of Remembrance

D - Book of Memorial

16) The following architectural styles are used in the legislature of the other provinces. Which of the following is not included?

A - Baroque

B - French Second Empire Style

C - Neoclassical

D - Romanesque

17) What is Canada's most popular spectator sport and is considered the national winter sport?

A - Polo

B - Basketball

C - Ice Skating

D - Hockey

18) When was Ice Hockey developed in Canada?
A - 1600s
B - 1700s
C - 1800s
D - 1900s

19) What is the name of the item that Lord Stanley donated in 1892 that the National Hockey League plays for?
A - Stanley Cup
B - Hockey Cup
C - Stanley Trophy
D - Hockey Trophy

20) What is the name of the cup that is awarded for women's hockey?
A - Women's Cup
B - Hockey Cup
C - Stanley Cup
D - Clarkson Cup

21) What is the 2nd most popular sport in Canada?
A - Basketball
B - Canadian Football
C - Polo
D - Lacrosse

22) What do you call the ice game introduced by Scottish pioneers?

A - Curling

B - Figure Ice Skating

C - Sledding

D - Skiing

23) What do you call the official summer sport that was first played by the Aboriginals?

A - Polo

B - Lacrosse

C - Swimming

D - Acrobats

24) What was adopted as a symbol of Hudson's Bay Company?

A - Hummingbird

B - Beaver

C - Koala

D - Raccoon

25) What French-Canadian patriotic association used the beaver as an emblem in 1834?

A - St. Jean Baptiste Society

B - St. Paul Society

C - St. Evangeline Society

D - St. Michael Society

26) At what age are applicants exempted from needing adequate knowledge in English or French to become a Canadian Citizen?

A - 45 years old

B - 55 years old

C - 65 years old

D - 75 years old

27) What is Canada's national anthem?

A - Hail Canada

B - Beloved Canada

C - Lovely Canada

D - O Canada

28) In what year was Canada's national anthem proclaimed?

A - 1870

B - 1980

C - 1990

D - 1890

29) Where was the national anthem first sung?

A - Quebec City

B - Toronto

C - Vancouver

D - Ottawa

30) What is the title of the Royal Anthem of Canada?

A - Royal Canada

B - God Save the King

C - O Canada

D - Beloved Canada

31) What did the jazz pianist Oscar Peterson receive from Roland Michener in 1973?

A - Order of Court

B - Medal of Valor

C - Victoria Cross

D - Order of Canada

32) What do official awards or honors consist of?

A - Orders

B - Decorations

C - Medals

D - All of the above

33) When was Canada's own honor system, the Order of Canada, started?

A - 1947

B - 1957

C - 1967

D - 1977

34) What do you call the highest honor available to Canadians?

A - Medal of Valor

B - Victoria Cross

C - Order of Canada

D - Medal of Honor

35) How many Canadians have been awarded the Victoria Cross, since 1854?

A - 66

B - 76

C - 86

D - 96

36) Who was the first Canadian to be awarded the Victoria Cross?

A - Corporal Filip Konowal

B - Lieutenant Robert Hampton Gray

C - Lieutenant Alexander Roberts Dunn

D - Captain Paul Triquet

37) Who was the first black male to be given the Victoria Cross?

A - Able Seaman William Hall

B - Lieutenant Robert Hampton Gray

C - Captain Paul Triquet

D - Lieutenant Alexander Roberts Dunn

38) Who was the flying ace that received the Victoria Cross during the First World War?

A - Lieutenant Alexander Roberts Dunn

B - Able Seaman William Hall

C - Captain Paul Triquet

D - Captain Billy Bishop

39) Who was the first member of the Canadian Corps not born inside the British Empire to be given the VC?

A - Captain Paul Triquet

B - Corporal Filip Konowal

C - Lieutenant Alexander Roberts Dunn

D - Able Seaman William Hall

40) When is Sir Wilfrid Laurier Day celebrated?

A - December 20

B - November 20

C - November 12
D - August 11

Canada's Economy (16 Questions)

1) When did Canada enact free trade with the United States?

A - 1968

B - 1978

C - 1988

D - 1998

2) What does NAFTA stand for?

A - North American Free Trade Agreement

B - North American Free Trade Associated

C - North Acadia Free Trade Agreement

D - North American Free Train Agreement

3) Which of the following is included in the three main types of Canada's industries?

A - Natural resources industries

B - Service industries

C - Manufacturing industries

D - All of the above

4) What % of Canadians now work in service industries?

A - 65%

B - 75%

C - 85%

D - 95%

5) Which of the following is not included in the Service industries?

A - Health care

B - Education

C - Transportation

D - Energy

6) Who is Canada's largest international trading partner?

A - United States

B - Britain

C - Australia

D - China

7) What do you call the border that Canadians and Americans cross every year in safety?

A - The world's longest undivided border

B - The world's longest undefended border

C - The world's longest unified border

D - The world's safest undefended border

8) Where can you find the words "children of common mother" inscribed?

A - Parliament Building

B - Statue of Liberty

C - Courts

D - Peace Arch

9) What does the Peace Arch symbolize?

A - Close ties and common interest

B - Freedom

C - Trade partner

D - None of the above

10) Where is the Peace Arch located?

A - Blaine in the State of Texas
B - Blaine in the State of Washington
C - Blaine in the State of Ohio
D - Blaine in the State of Illinois

11) What is the estimated Canadian export destined for the U.S.A?
A - Three-quarters
B - Two-thirds
C - Half
D - One-quarter

12) What remains as the engine of Canada's economic growth?
A - Mining
B - Fishery
C - Logging
D - Commerce

13) Which country became a partner in 1994 as part of the broader North American Free Trade Agreement (NAFTA)?
A - Paris
B - Mexico
C - Russia
D - Japan

14) What type of dam can be found in Saguenay River, Quebec?
A - Hydro-Electric Dam
B - Diversion Dam
C - Coffer Dam

D - Industrial Waste Dam

15) Which industry makes products to sell in Canada and around the world?

A - Service

B - Manufacturing

C - Shipping

D - Natural resources

16) Which of the following is included in the manufactured products that Canada sells?

A - Automobiles

B - Paper

C - Aerospace technology

D - All of the above

Canada's Regions (105 Questions)

1) What is Canada known as?
   A - 3rd largest country on earth
   B - 4th largest country on earth
   C - 2nd largest country on earth
   D - 5th largest country on earth

2) How many oceans line Canada's frontier?
   A - 2
   B - 3
   C - 4
   D - 5

3) What is the ocean that lines Canada's frontier to the east?
   A - Indian
   B - Pacific
   C - Atlantic
   D - Arctic

4) What is the ocean that lines Canada's frontier to the north?
   A - Atlantic
   B - Indian
   C - Pacific
   D - Arctic

5) What is the ocean that lines Canada's frontier to the west?
   A - Arctic
   B - Pacific

C - Indian

D - Atlantic

6) How many regions does Canada have?

A - 5

B - 6

C - 7

D - 8

7) Which of the following is part of Canada's Regions?

A - Central Canada

B - The West Coast

C - The Northern Territories

D - All of the above

8) In what year was Ottawa chosen as the capital?

A - 1997

B - 1857

C - 1700

D - 1888

9) What is Canada's fourth largest metropolitan area?

A - Vancouver

B - Toronto

C - Ottawa

D - New Brunswick

10) Who decided on Ottawa as the capital in 1857?
A - Queen Victoria
B - Frederic
C - Nunavut
D - Ontario

11) How many square kilometers is the National Capital Region surrounding Ottawa?
A - 4,500 square kilometers
B - 3,700 square kilometers
C - 5,000 square kilometers
D - 4,700 square kilometers

12) How many Provinces does Canada have?
A - 11
B - 9
C - 10
D - 15

13) How many territories does Canada have?
A - 3
B - 4
C - 5
D - 6

14) What do each province and territory in Canada have?
A - Court
B - Parliament
C - Land measurement
D - Capital City

15) **What is the estimated count of Canada's population?**
   A - 44 million
   B - 34 million
   C - 15 million
   D - 47 million

16) **What is the name of a now tourist attraction and winter skateway that was once a military waterway?**
   A - Ottawa's Great Canal
   B - Ontario's Rideau Canal
   C - Ottawa's Rideau Canal
   D - Ontario's Great Canal

17) **What is the Capital City of Ontario Province?**
   A - Ottawa
   B - Vancouver
   C - Toronto
   D - Quebec

18) **Which of the following is not part of Prairie Provinces?**
   A - Saskatchewan
   B - British Columbia
   C - Alberta
   D - Manitoba

19) **What is the Capital City of British Columbia?**
   A - Victoria

B - Charlottetown

C - Fredericton

D - Winnipeg

20) Which of the following is not included in Atlantic Provinces?

A - British Columbia

B - Manitoba

C - Nunavut

D - All of the above

21) What is New Brunswick's Capital City?

A - Winnipeg

B - Fredericton

C - Nunavut

D - Alberta

22) What is Prince Edward Island's Capital City?

A - Alberta

B - Fredericton

C - Winnipeg

D - Charlottetown

23) St. John's is the capital city of what province?

A - Nova Scotia

B - New Brunswick

C - Newfoundland and Labrador

D - Quebec

24) Fredericton is the capital city of what province?

A - Quebec

B - New Brunswick

C - Nova Scotia

D - Nunavut

25) Regina is the capital city of what province?

A - Saskatchewan

B - Nova Scotia

C - Nunavut

D - Alberta

26) Manitoba is part of what province?

A - Atlantic Provinces

B - West Coast

C - Prairie provinces

D - Central Canada

27) Nova Scotia is part of what province?

A - Central Canada

B - West Coast

C - Prairie provinces

D - Atlantic provinces

28) Which of the following is not Canada's territory?

A - Northwest Territories

B - Southwest Territories

C - Yukon Territory

D - Nunavut

29) Where is the most easterly point in Northern America that has its own time zone?

A - Newfoundland and Labrador

B - British Columbia

C - Nunavut

D - Prince Edward Island

30) What is the smallest province that is known for its beaches, red soil, and agriculture, especially potatoes?

A - British Columbia

B - Saskatchewan

C - Manitoba

D - Prince Edward Island

31) What does the province of Labrador have immensely?

A - Ship manufacturing

B - Hydro-electric resources

C - Fishery

D - Mining

32) What do you call the bridge that connects Prince Edward Island to mainland Canada?

A - San Juanico Bridge

B - Golden Gate Bridge

C - Confederation Bridge

D - Canada Bridge

THE CANADIAN CITIZENSHIP TEST

33) What is the title of the fable about the happenings of a red-headed orphan girl by Lucy Maud Montgomery that was set in Prince Edward Island?

A - Anna Banana

B - Anne of Green Gables

C - Princess Sarah

D - Princess Diaries

34) What is the most populated Atlantic Province and a gateway to Canada?

A - Nova Scotia

B - Alberta

C - Saskatchewan

D - Manitoba

35) What is Nova Scotia's Capital City?

A - Winnipeg

B - Alberta

C - Halifax

D - Edmonton

36) The following are part of Nova Scotia's identity except for one, which is it?

A - Mining

B - Fisheries

C - Shipbuilding

D - Shipping

37) What tradition sustains a vibrant culture in Nova Scotia?

A - French tradition

B - Aboriginal traditional

C - Celtic and Gaelic tradition

D - Irish tradition

38) What is Halifax home to?

A - Fishery

B - Coal mining

C - Ship building

D - Canada's largest naval base

39) How many annual festivals does Nova Scotia hold?

A - Over 800

B - Over 500

C - Over 700

D - Over 600

40) What is the province that was founded by United Empire Loyalists and also has the 2nd largest river system on North America's Atlantic coastline?

A - Manitoba

B - Nunavut

C - New Brunswick

D - Alberta

41) What do you call the 2nd biggest river system on North America's Atlantic coastline?

A - St. John River system

B - North America River system

C - Canada River system

D - Atlantic River system

42) Which of the following is New Brunswick's principal industry?
A - Agriculture
B - Forestry
C - Mining
D - All of the above

43) What is New Brunswick's principal Francophone Acadian center?
A - Vancouver
B - Ottawa
C - Moncton
D - Manitoba

44) What is New Brunswick's largest city, port, and manufacturing center?
A - Manitoba
B - Saint John
C - Moncton
D - Vancouver

45) What do you call the area near the Great Lakes/St. Lawrence River in southern Quebec and Ontario?
A - Main Canada
B - Great Lakes Canada
C - St. John River
D - Central Canada

46) Which provinces produce more than 3/4 of all Canadian manufactured goods?
A - Ontario and Manitoba
B - Ontario and Quebec
C - Quebec and Alberta
D - Quebec and Regina

47) What kind of winters and summers do Ontario and Quebec have?
A - Cold winters and warm humid summer
B - Harsh winter and dry summer
C - Mild winter and humid summer
D - Cold winter and cool summer

48) Which province is Canada's main producer of pulp and paper?
A - Ontario
B - Manitoba
C - Regina
D - Quebec

49) What is Quebec known for, having a huge supply of fresh water?
A - Canada's largest producer of naval ships
B - Canada's largest producer of hydroelectricity
C - Canada's largest fishery
D - Canada's largest producer of dams

50) What is Canada's 2nd largest city and the 2nd largest French-speaking city in the world behind Paris?
A - Manitoba

B - Regina

C - Montreal

D – Edmonton

51) What is the largest city in Canada and also the country's main financial center?

A - Vancouver

B - Montreal

C - Halifax

D - Toronto

52) What is known for its vineyards, wines, waterfall, and fruit crops?

A - Halifax

B - Yukon Territory

C - Alberta

D - Niagara Region

53) Which of the following do Ontario farmers raise?

A - Poultry

B - Dairy and beef cattle

C - Vegetable and grain crops

D - All of the above

54) How many lakes are there located between Ontario and the United States?

A - 4

B - 5

C - 6

D - 7

55) Which of these is the largest freshwater lake in the world?
A - Lake Superior
B - Grand Lake
C - Lake Erie
D - Lake Huron

56) What is the name of the province whose economy relies on agriculture, mining, and hydro-electric generation, with Winnipeg as the most populated city?
A - Ottawa
B - Saskatchewan
C - Ontario
D - Manitoba

57) What is the most famous street intersection in Canada?
A - Montage and Main
B - Portage and Main
C - Fountain and Main
D - Porridge and Main

58) What do you call Winnipeg's French Quarter that has Western Canada's largest Francophone community?
A - St. John's
B - St. Paul
C - St. Boniface
D - St. Andrew's

59) What is the estimated percentage of people with Ukrainian origins living in Manitoba?

A - 14%
B - 15%
C - 16%
D - 17%

60) What is the estimated percentage of Aboriginal populations living in Manitoba?
A - 14%
B - 15%
C - 16%
D - 17%

61) The province of Saskatchewan was known as what?
A - Bed and breakfast of the world
B - Breadbasket of the world
C - Rice province
D - None cf the above

62) Saskatchewan is the country's largest producer of what?
A - Coal
B - Rice
C - Fish
D - Grains and oilseed

63) What is Saskatchewan rich in?
A - Grain
B - Uranium and potash
C - Manure
D - None of the above

64) What is Saskatchewan's largest city and the center of the mining industry?

A - Ottawa

B - Nunavut

C - Regina

D - Saskatoon

65) Regina, the capital of Saskatchewan, is home to the training academy of which police force?

A - Uniformed Patrol Officers

B - Royal Canadian Mounted Police

C - Transit and railroad police

D - Municipal Police

66) What is the most populous Prairie province?

A - Saskatchewan

B - Alberta

C - Manitoba

D - Ontario

67) Where did Alberta and Lake Louise get their names?

A - From Queen Victoria

B - From the Prime Minister

C - From the Aboriginals

D - Princess Louise Caroline Alberta

68) How many national parks does Alberta have?

A - 5

B - 8

C - 6

D - 4

69) When was Banff National Park established?

A - 1889

B - 1985

C - 1990

D - 1885

70) Alberta is the largest producer of what?

A - Grain

B - Coal

C - Oil and gas

D - Hydro-electric

71) What is Alberta renowned for that makes Canada one of the world's major beef producers?

A - Large import of beefs

B - Vast cattle ranches

C - A lot of green pastures

D - None of the above

72) What is British Columbia known as?

A - Canada's Pacific gateway

B - British Columbia bridge

C - St. John's gateway

D - British Columbia gateway

73) What is Canada's largest and busiest port, which also handles billions of dollars in goods traded around the world?
A - British Columbia port
B - West Coast port
C - Port of Vancouver
D - Pacific port

74) Which has the most expensive park system in Canada?
A - British Columbia
B - Ontario
C - Alberta
D - Vancouver

75) What is the approximate number of parks that British Columbia has?
A - Approximately 400 provincial parks
B - Approximately 500 provincial parks
C - Approximately 600 provincial parks
D - Approximately 700 provincial parks

76) What are the most spoken languages in British Columbia after English?
A - French and Punjabi
B - Chinese and Punjabi
C - Tagalog and Chinese
D - Chinese and Irish

77) The capital city Victoria, is a tourist center and base of what fleet?
A - Marine's Pacific Fleet

B - Canada's Atlantic Fleet

C - Navy's Atlantic Fleet

D - Navy's Pacific Fleet

78) These northwestern territories contain 1/3 of Canada's land mass - but only have a population of around 100,000 people.

A - Nunavut and Yukon

B - Nunavut and Northwest

C - Yukon and Ontario

D - Quebec and Nunavut

79) What is the north often referred to as?

A - Land of the Midnight Sun

B - Land of the Morning Sun

C - Land of the North

D - Northern Star

80) In the height of summer, how long can the daylight last in the north?

A - 16 hours

B - 20 hours

C - 24 hours

D - 12 hours

81) In winter, how many months does the sun disappear and darkness sets in for?

A - 4 months

B - 3 months

C - 7 months

D - 10 months

82) Large areas of the north are made up of what?
A - Frost
B - Forrest
C - Tundra
D - Pasture

83) What do the people of the north commonly do to earn a living?
A - Fishing
B - Hunting
C - Farming
D - Trapping

84) Which of the following mines are found in the north?
A - Lead
B - Gold
C - Zinc
D - All of the above

85) During what event did thousands of miners come to Yukon?
A - Silver Rush of the 1990s
B - Gold Rush of the 1890s
C - Diamond Rush of 1870s
D - Copper Rush of 1880s

86) What opened from Skagway in neighboring Alaska to the territorial capital, Whitehorse, which provides a tourist expedition across risky passes and bridges?

A - White Pass and Yukon Railway
B - Alaska Pass and Yukon Train
C - Whitehorse Pass and Alaska Trail
D - Alaska Pass and Yukon Train

87) In which year was the pass and railway opened?
A - 1700
B - 1600
C - 1800
D - 1900

88) Yukon holds the bragging rights for the coldest temperature on record in Canada, at what temperature?
A - (-83°C)
B - (-63°C)
C - (-53°C)
D - (-73°C)

89) What is the highest mountain in Canada?
A - Mount Canada
B - Mount Everest
C - Mount Yukon
D - Mount Logan

90) Who is the world-famous geologist in which the highest mountain in Canada was named after?
A - Sir William Logan
B - Sir Wilbert Logan

C - Sir Wilson Logan
D - Sir Wilfred Logan

91) What was formed from "Rupert's Land" and the North-Western Territory in 1870?
A - Northeast Territories
B - North-South Territories
C - Northwest Territories (N.W.T)
D - None of the Above

92) What is the name of the capital that is called the diamond capital of North America?
A - Yellowstone
B - Yellowknife
C - Red Valley
D - Redstone

93) What is the second-longest river in North America (after the Mississippi)?
A - Canada River
B - St. John's River
C - Mackenzie River
D - Nile River

94) What does Nunavut mean in Inuktitut?
A - Our land
B - Our community
C - Our farm
D - Our people

95) In what year was Nunavut established?

A - 1980
B - 1976
C - 1996
D - 1999

96) What is the capital of Nunavut?
A - Iqaluit
B - Yellowknife
C - Ontario
D - Regina

97) What was the capital formerly known as?
A - Inuit Bay
B - Fortune Bay
C - Frobisher Bay
D - Fisher's Bay

98) Who was the capital (Frobisher Bay) named after?
A - Mark Frobisher
B - Marco Frobisher
C - Marcel Frobisher
D - Martin Frobisher

99) What is the official language of Nunavut and the first language in schools?
A - Michif
B - Inuktitut
C - Aboriginal
D - Metis

100) How does the 19-member Legislative Assembly choose a premier and ministers?

A - By consensus

B - By debate

C - By hunting

D - From the Prime Minister's suggestion

101)   Who deals with the harsh weather conditions in an isolated region to secure and keep the flag flying in Canada's Arctic?

A - Canadian Rangers

B - Royal Canadian Mounted Police

C - Governor-General

D - Mayor

102)   Canadian Rangers are part of what police force?

A - Royal Canadian Mounted Police

B - Canada's National Police Force

C - Canadian Forces Reserves (militia)

D - Railway Police

103)   What do the Rangers use to travel during winter?

A - Sled

B - Ski

C - Snowmobile

D - Tram

104) **What do you call the popular game for hunters, and a symbol of Canada's North?**

A - Caribou

B - Hockey

C - Basketball

D - Skating

105) **What is a Caribou?**

A - Raccoon

B - Eagle

C - Beaver

D - Reindeer

True or False Questions

1) True or False, Canada is part of the United States.

2) True or False, Canadians cannot leave the country freely.

3) True or False, Habeas Corpus is derived from French common law.

4) True or False, Aboriginal People have rights.

5) True or False, mobility rights are a fundamental characteristic of Canadian heritage and identity.

6) True or False, The Constitution of Canada was changed in 1982.

7) True or False, the Prime Minister of Canada is above the law.

8) True or False, voting rights give citizens the responsibility to vote in federal, provincial, or territorial and local elections.

9) True or False, all citizens should protect Canada's natural, cultural, and architectural heritage for the future.

10) True or False, joining the military service is forced in Canada.

11) True or False, Canada is known for being a strong and free country.

12) True or False, Canada is the only Constitutional Monarch in the world.

13) True or False, Canada's original constitutional document was formed in 1864.

14) True or False, many poets/songwriters have hailed Canada as the Great Land.

15) True or False, Canada has five founding groups.

16) True or False, the ancestors of Aboriginal people are thought to have migrated from Australia.

17) True or False, territorial rights were first granted through the Royal Proclamation by Queen Elizabeth II.

18) True or False, the government put Aboriginal children in residential schools to incorporate them into Canadian culture, while Aboriginal practices were prohibited.

19) True or False, the term Aboriginal peoples refers to three distinct groups: Indian, Inuit, and Métis/Inuit.

20) True or False, Inuit means "the people" in the Michif language.

21) True or False, the Métis mostly live in the Prairies.

22) True or False, roughly 65% of Aboriginal people are First Nations, while 30% are Métis, and 4% are Inuit.

23) True or False, the Acadians are descendants of French colonists who began settling in Canada in 1604.

24) True or False, the war where Arcadians were deported from their homeland is known as the Great Ordeal.

25) True or False, people who speak French as their first language are called Anglophones.

26) True or False, English speakers are called Anglophones.

27) True or False, the Prime Minister recognized that Quebecois formed a nation within united Canada.

28) True or False, Canada's diversity does not include gay and lesbians.

29) True or False, most Canadians identify as Christian.

30) True or False, the first explorers of Canada thought they reached the East Indies.

31) True or False, John Cabot was an English immigrant to Canada.

32) True or False, Jacques Cartier was the first European to find what we now call Québec City and Montreal.

33) True or False, in the 1550s, the word Canada first appeared on maps.

34) True or False, Pierre de Monts/Samuel de Champlain were Italian explorers.

35) True or False, the fur-trade was driven by the need for raccoon pelts in Europe.

36) True or False, The Quebec Act of 1774 allowed gender freedom.

37) True or False, The Quebec Act also restored French civil law while keeping British criminal law.

38) True or False, King Charles II granted the Hudson's Bay Company exclusive rights for watershed draining in 1770 - effectively creating a monopoly.

39) True or False, in 1759, the British overpowered the French in the "Battle of the Plains."

40) True or False, in 1792, black Nova Scotians established Scottown in Sierra Leone.

41) True or False, The Constitutional Act of 1791 gave way for the name Canada to become official.

42) True or False, the first companies in Canada were formed during competition over mining.

43) True or False, The Provincial Freeman is a newspaper focused on women's rights.

44) True or False, Montreal's Stock Exchange opened officially in 1832.

45) True or False, in 1814, Robert Ross led an event where the White house was set on fire and burned down.

46) True or False, armed rebels were defeated by Irish troops and Canadian volunteers in 1837-38, outside of Montreal and Toronto.

47) True or False, Lord Durham said the best way for the Canadians to achieve progress was to take part in Muslim culture.

48) True or False, Nova Scotia attained full responsible government in 1847-1848.

49) True or False, until 1982, July 1 was called "Dominion Day" - now, however, it is known as Canada Day.

50) True or False, Prime Minister Trudeau established the North West Mounted Police force.

51) True or False, British Columbia joined Canada when Ottawa promised to build a bridge to the West.

52) True or False, Ottawa formed the Canadian Expeditionary Force in 1914.

53) True or False, Sir Arthur Currie was known as Canada's greatest soldier.

54) True or False, Dr. Emily Stowe was the first Canadian lady to work professionally in medicine in Canada.

55) True or False, Remembrance Day takes place on November 21st, every year.

56) True or False, Canada's Central Bank was formed in 1934.

57) True or False, Canadians captured Juno Beach in the 1st World War.

58) True or False, The Canadian Army helped free the Netherlands in 1945.

59) True or False, The Royal Canadian Navy protected merchant ships from German submarines.

60) True or False, the cold war was initiated by the Soviet Union - under dictator Josef Stalin.

61) True or False, the push for Quebec sovereignty was overpowered in 1930.

62) True or False, Dr. Wilfred Penfield was known as the greatest living Canadian.

63) True or False, the federal government takes responsibility for matters like defense, currency, and citizenship.

64) True or False, the Parliament has two distinct parts - the Sovereign and the House of Commons.

65) True or False, the Prime Minister in office chooses the Cabinet ministers.

66) True or False, the three northern territories (Yukon, Northwest Territories, and

Nunavut) don't have the status of provinces.

67) True or False, the Governor directs the governing of Canada.

68) True or False, in the three Northern territories, the mayor has a ceremonial role.

69) True or False, everyone in the electoral district can vote for the party of their choice.

70) True or False, the Prime Minister decides the Crown ministers.

71) True or False, after an election, the PM is appointed by the Governor General.

72) True or False, right now, there are three main parties - the Conservatives, New Democrats, and the Liberals.

73) True or False, the Prime Minister and Cabinet ministers, together, are referred to as the shelf.

74) True or False, the Voter Information Card confirms that you are on the list of voters and states who you voted for.

75) True or False, provincial, territorial, and municipal elections have the same rules as federal elections.

76) True or False, The First Nations have responsibilities including housing & schools.

77) True or False, the legal system is formed upon the rule of law, democratic principles, and due process, amongst other things.

78) True or False, freedom under the law is the principle where the government must respect a person's legal rights.

79) True or False, you can question the police about their service or conduct.

80) True or False, the Crown has been the symbol of French royalty for more than 1,000 years.

81) True or False, the beaver is Canada's best-known symbol.

82) True or False, many young Canadians play hockey at school.

83) True or False, The Royal Anthem of Canada (God Save the King) can be when Canadians want to honor the sovereign.

84) True or False, November 30th is the day of Sir Wilfrid Laurier.

85) True or False, today, Canada is part of the G8.

86) True or False, greater than 75% of Canadians work in service-based industries.

87) True or False, Ottawa is Canada's largest metropolitan area.

88) True or False, Nova Scotia has a history of hydro-electric dams.

89) True or False, New Brunswick is <u>officially the only</u> bilingual province of Canada.

90) True or False, Quebecers are leaders in industries such as pharmaceuticals and electronics.

91) True or False, Manitoba is the center of Ukrainian life in Canada, with 14% of the population having Ukrainian origin.

92) True or False, Alberta is the biggest producer of oil and gas (O&G) in Canada.

93) True or False, half of all the goods produced in British Columbia are dairy products.

94) True or False, there are trees on the tundra.

95) True or False, Wilson Logan is one of Canada's greatest scientists.

96) True or False, more than 50% of the population in the Northwest Territories are Aboriginal.

97) True or False, Michif is an official and the first school language in Nunavut.

98) True or False, The Badlands of Ontario are home to prehistoric fossils and dinosaur relics.

99) True or False, Yukon's Capital is Whitehorse.

100) True or False, Canada is the third largest country on earth.

Rights & Responsibilities (Answers)

1) Which year was the Magna Carta signed and introduced?
A - 1786
B - 1315
C - 1215
D - 1777

The answer is C, 1215

2) Which of these is not part of the Magna Carta?
A - Freedom of Conscience & Religion
B - Freedom of Speech
C - Freedom of Eating
D - Freedom of Association

The answer is C, Freedom of Eating!

3) When was the constitution of Canada amended?
A - 1982
B - 1992
C - 2002
D - 2022

The answer is A, 1982.

4) **What do you call the Right where the English and the French have equal status in the Parliament and the government?**
A - Information Rights
B - Multiculturalism
C - Official Language Rights
D - Aboriginal Peoples' Rights

The answer is C, Official Language Rights

5) **What do you call a person's right to challenge unlawful detention by the state?**
A - Canadian Charter Rights
B - Habeas Corpus
C - Magna Carta
D - Habeas Corpus

The answer is D, Habeas Corpus

6) **What do you call the Right where Canadians can live and work freely anywhere in Canada, apply for a passport, and leave the country freely?**
A - Aboriginal Peoples' Rights
B - Mobility Rights
C - Magna Carta
D - Official Language Rights and Minority Language Educational Rights

The answer is B, Mobility Rights

7) Where was the constitution amended and proclaimed?

A - Tokyo

B - Ottawa

C - Vancouver

D - Toronto

The answer is B, Ottawa

8) Complete the sentence, "Whereas Canada is founded upon _____ that recognize the supremacy of God, as well as the rule of _____."

A - Principles, Law

B - Principal, Order

C - Truth, Law

D - Truth, Order

The answer is A, Principles and Law

9) What do you call the Right in which Canadians celebrate the gift of each other's presence, respect pluralism, and live in harmony?

A - Aboriginal Peoples' Rights

B - Mobility Rights

C - Habeas Corpus

D - Multiculturalism

The answer is D, Multiculturalism

10) Which of these best describe Aboriginal Peoples' Rights?

A - They have no rights

B - Their rights and freedoms should be respected

C - They have more rights than the French

D - They have more rights than everyone

The answer is B, the rights guaranteed that it will not affect any treaty, other rights or freedom of the Aboriginal People

11) Which of the following acts does Canadian criminal law not tolerate?

A - Gender-based Violence

B - Spousal Abuse

C - Forced Marriage

D - All of the above

The answer is D, All of the above

12) Which of the below is a responsibility of a citizen?

A - Serving on a jury

B - Obeying the law

C - Voting

D - All of the above

The answer is D, All of the above

13) **No person/group is above the law. What is this responsibility called?**

A - Serving on a jury

B - Habeas Corpus

C - Obeying the law

D - Protecting and enjoying the heritage

The answer is C, Obeying the law

14) **Is joining the military required in Canada?**

A - Yes

B - No

C - Yes, but with exemptions

D - Depends on the situation

The answer is B, joining the military is **not** required in Canada

15) **What do you call the citizenship responsibility where you are required to vote in federal, provincial, and local elections?**

A - Voting

B - Multiculturalism

C - Serving on a jury

D - Obeying the law

The answer is A, Voting

16) A citizenship responsibility in which you shall respect and protect Canada's cultural, natural, and architectural heritage is called what?

A - Multiculturalism

B - Helping others in the community

C - Obeying the law

D - Protecting and enjoying our heritage and environment

The answer is D, Protecting and enjoying our heritage and environment

17) Why is it important to serve on a jury as part of citizenship responsibility?

A - It avoids waste and pollution

B - It is easy

C - It's a privilege as the justice system relies on the impartial and unbiased jurors for it to work

D - It doesn't last long

The answer is C, It's a privilege as the justice system relies on the impartial and unbiased jurors for it to work

18) Which of the following can you join as a way to serve and contribute to Canada?

A - Navy

B - Army

C - Air Force

D - All of the above

The answer is D, All of the above

19) What can you learn when you join the Canadian Forces?

A - Discipline

B - Responsibility

C - Skills

D - All of the Above

The answer is D, All of the above

20) What do you call the citizenship responsibility in which you help other people in your community by volunteering?

A - Obeying the law

B - Helping others in the community

C - Protecting the heritage

D - Taking responsibility for oneself and one's family

The answer is B, Helping others in the community

Who We Are (Answers)

1) Who are the founding people of Canada?
A - French
B - Aboriginal
C - British
D - All of the above

The answer is D, All of the above

2) What is Canada known as around the world?
A - Strong and Independent Country
B - Strong and Free Country
C - Independent and Free Country
D - None of the above

The answer is B, a Strong and Free country

3) Canada is the only country with what kind of government in North America?
A - Constitutional monarchy
B - Federalism
C - Democracy
D - Dictatorship

The answer is A, Constitutional monarchy

4) The institution upholds a commitment to which of the following?
A - Peace
B - Order

C - Good Government

D - All of the above

The answer is D, All of the above

5) What did poets and songwriters hail Canada as?

A - Great Denomination

B - Grand Dominion

C - Great Dominion

D - Grand Denomination

The answer is C, Great Dominion

6) What do you call the 1867 constitutional document in which Peace, Order, and Good Government was used as a key phrase?

A - Magna Carta

B - Royal Proclamation

C - Canadian Charter of Rights and Freedom

D - British North America Act

The answer is D, British North America Act

7) Where were the ancestors of the Aboriginal people believed to have migrated from?

A - Europe

B - Asia

C - France

D - America

The answer is B, Asia

8) From what period in time did the government place aboriginal children in residential schools to help educate them?

A - 1800s until 2000s

B - 1800s until 1980s

C - 1970s until 1980s

D - 1700s until 1800s

The answer is B, 1800s until 1980s

9) Who was the monarch that signed the Royal Proclamation of 1763?

A - King George III

B - King George IV

C - Queen Victoria

D - Queen Elizabeth

The answer is A, King George III

10) What do you call the right that was guaranteed through the Royal Proclamation of 1763?

A - Magna Carta

B - Great Charter of Freedom

C - Territorial Rights

D - Canadian Charter of Rights and Freedom

The answer is C, Territorial Rights

11) What does the term *Aboriginal people* refer to in today's world?

A - Indian, Inuit, and Mètis

B - Indian, Irish, and Mètis

C - English, Inuit, and Mètis

D - None of the above

The answer is A, Indian, Inuit, and Mètis.

12) Which of these were mostly prohibited in the residential schools that the federal government established during the 1800s-1980s?

A - French languages

B - English languages

C - Aboriginal languages and cultural practices

D - None of the above

The answer is C, Aboriginal languages and cultural practices

13) In what year did Ottawa formally apologize to the former students who were abused?

A - 2005

B - 2006

C - 2007

D - 2008

The answer is D, 2008

14) When did the term "First Nations" begin to be used?

A - 1700s

B - 1890s

C - 1950s

D - 1970s

The answer is D, 1970s

15) Who was the 1st Baron Tweedsmuir as well as the popular Governor General of Canada from 1935 to 1940?

A - John Buchon

B - Eric Buchan

C - Eric Buchon

D - John Buchan

The answer is D, John Buchan

16) What do you call the Aboriginal people who live in small scattered communities in the Arctic?

A - Inuit

B - Mètis

C - Indian

D - Icelander

The answer is A, Inuit

17) Where do the majority of Mètis people live?

A - Central Canada

B - Prairie Provinces

C - North Territories

D - None of the above

The answer is B, Prairie Provinces

18) What do you call the dialect that the Mètis people speak?

A - Inuktitut

B - Michif

C - Mètisians

D - Aboriginal

The answer is B, Michif

19) What does Inuit mean in the Inuktitut language?

A - The friends

B - The people

C - The country

D - The community

The answer is B, The people

20) The Mètis are the descendants of what mixed ancestry?

A - Aboriginal and European

B - European and Indian

C - Irish and Indian

D - Indian and Aboriginal

The answer is A, Aboriginal and European ancestry

21) What are the official languages of Canada?

A - English and Chinese

B - French and Irish

C - English and French

D - French and Chinese

The answer is C, English and French

22) What do you call people who use English as their first language?

A - Francophones

B - Anglophones

C - Bilinguals

D - None of the above

The answer is B, Anglophones

23) What do you call people who use French as their first language?

A - Anglophones

B - English

C - Bilingual

D - Francophones

The answer is D, Francophones

24) What is the only official province which is bilingual?

A - Ottawa

B - Toronto

C - New Brunswick

D - Vancouver

The answer is C, New Brunswick

25) What do you call the event that happened during the 1700s where most Acadians were deported from their homeland?

A - Great Upheaval

B - Great Uproar

C - Grand Upheaval

D - Grand Uproar

The answer is A, Great Upheaval

26) When did the House of Commons recognize the Quebecois as a formed nation within a united Canada?

A - 2010

B - 2006

C - 1900

D - 2000

The answer is B, 2006

27) What do Anglophones generally refer to themselves as?

A - English Aboriginal

B - Aboriginal Canadian

C - French Canadian

D - English Canadian

The answer is D, English Canadian

28) Who established the basic way of life in the English-speaking area?

A - English, Welsh, Scottish, and Irish settlers

B - English, Welsh, Indian, and Irish settlers

C - French, Welsh, Scottish, and Irish settlers

D - None of the Above

The answer is A, English, Welsh, Scottish, and Irish settlers

29) What did you call people of Quebec?

A - Quebec

B - Inuit

C - Quebecers

D - English

The answer is C, Quebecers

30) What is the estimated count of English and French speakers as of today?

A - 20 million Anglophones, 8 million Francophones

B - 18 million Anglophones, 8 million Francophones

C - 20 million Anglophones, 7 million Francophones

D - 18 million Anglophones, 7 million Francophones

The answer is D, 18 million Anglophones and 7 million Francophones

31) What is Canada often referred to as?

A - Land of Settlers

B - Land of Immigrants

C - State of Immigrants

D - State of Settlers

The answer is B, Land of Immigrants

32) What is the second most-spoken language in Vancouver and Toronto?

A - Indian language

B - French language

C - Korean language

D - Chinese language

The answer is D, Chinese language

33) What is the largest religious affiliation in Canada?

A - Catholic

B - Protestant

C - Muslim

D - Jews

The answer is A, Catholic

34) Why did Canada partner with faith communities?

A - To help promote social welfare

B - To help provide schools and healthcare

C - To help resettle refugees

D - All of the above

The answer is D, All of the above

35) Which of the following is also included in Canada's diversity?

A - Young and old Canadians

B - Gay and lesbian Canadians

C - Immigrants and soldiers

D - None of the above

The answer is B, Gay and lesbian Canadians

36) What is the estimated percentage of the population that speaks Chinese at home in Vancouver?

A - 43% of the population

B - 15% of the population

C - 13% of the population

D - 33% of the population

The answer is C, 13% of the population

37) What is the estimated percentage of the population that speaks Chinese at home in Toronto?

A - 7% of the population

B - 17% of the population

C - 0.7% of the population

D - 27% of the population

The answer is A, 7% of the population

38) Who is the Olympian that is a descendant of Black Loyalists, escaped slaves and freed men and women of American origin - who in the 1970s fled to Canada from America?

A - Abigail Strait

B - Marjorie Turner-Bailey

C - Vasek Pospisil

D - Piper Gilles

The answer is B, Marjorie Turner-Bailey

39) In the 1970s, most immigrants came from what countries?

A - Australia

B - European

C - Asian

D - America

The answer is C, Asian

40) New Canadians are expected to embrace democratic principles such as what?

A - Rule of community

B - Rule of land

C - Rule of monarchy

D - Rule of law

The answer is D, Rule of law

Canada's History (Answers)

1) Who were the natives occupying the region that the Europeans found when they explored Canada?

A - Asians

B - Indians

C - Irish

D - Americans

The answer is B, Indians

2) Why were the natives called Indians?

A - Because the Europeans saw their clothing style

B - Because the Europeans thought they had reached the North Indies

C - Because the Europeans noticed the different settlement

D - Because the Europeans thought they had reached the East Indies

The answer is D, Because the Europeans thought they had reached the East Indies

3) What do you call the native people of the Great Lakes region?

A - Inuit

B - Aboriginal

C - Huron-Wendat

D - Nomads

The answer is C, Huron-Wendat

4) **What were the native people of the Northwest, Cree and Dene?**
   A - Hunter-gatherers
   B - Fishermen
   C - Farmers
   D - Software Developers

The answer is A, Hunter-gatherers

5) **How do West Coast natives preserve fish?**
   A - By deboning
   B - By drying and smoking
   C - By using salt
   D - By preserving in a jar

The answer is B, By drying and smoking

6) **What is common among aboriginal groups as they compete for land, resources, and prestige?**
   A - Trading
   B - Business
   C - Farming
   D - Warfare

The answer is D, Warfare

7) **Why did a large number of aboriginal people die of European diseases?**
   A - Because they lacked immunity
   B - Because of huge volume of settlers
   C - Because of poor hygiene
   D - None of the above

The answer is A, Because they lacked immunity

8) **What did the Aboriginals and Europeans form that laid the foundation of Canada?**

A - Economic Bonds

B - Religious Bonds

C - Military Bonds

D - All of the above

The answer is D, All of the above

9) **Who was the first person to map out Canada's East Coast?**

A - Peter Cabot

B - John Cabot

C - Peter John

D - John Shore

The answer is B, John Cabot

10) **Who was the first European to explore St. Lawrence River and discover present-day Quebec City and Montreal?**

A - Jacques Cabot

B - Henry Cartier

C - Henry Cabot

D - Jacques Cartier

The answer is D, Jacques Cartier

11) **Where did the Vikings who colonized Greenland come from?**

A - Ireland

B - Iceland

C - The Arctic

D - Canada

The answer is B, Iceland

12) What do you call the remains of the settlement of Vikings who colonized Greenland, which is a World Heritage site today?

A - l'Anse aux Meadows

B - The Ships

C - The Lost Town

D - The Eiffel Tower

The answer is A, l'Anse aux Meadows

13) When did European exploration begin?

A - 1500

B - 1978

C - 1497

D - 1450

The answer is C, 1497

14) How many voyages did Jacques Cartier make between 1534 and 1542?

A - Two

B - Three

C - Four

D - Five

The answer is B, Three

15) What does the Iroquoian word Kanata mean?

A - People

B - Settlers

C - Community

D - Village

The answer is D, Village

16) When did the word Canada begin appearing on maps?

A - 1600s

B - 1670s

C - 1550s

D - 1480s

The answer is C, 1550s

17) Who refused to surrender Quebec to England in 1690?

A - Count Pierre

B - Count Frontenac

C - Sir Guy Carleton

D - Lord Dochester

The answer is B, Count Frontenac

18) Who was the Governor of Quebec who defended the rights of Canadians?

A - Count Frontenac

B - Henry Cabot

C - Jacques Cartier

D - Sir Guy Carleton

The answer is D, Sir Guy Carleton

19) In what year did Sir Guy Carleton defeat an American military invasion of Quebec?
    A - 1775
    B - 1780
    C - 1890
    D - 1875

The answer is A, 1775

20) Who were the French explorers who established the first European settlement north of Florida?
    A - Pierre de Monts and Samuel de Champlain
    B - Pierre de Champlain and Samuel de Monts
    C - Pierre de Cartier and Samuel de Monts
    D - Pierre de Champlain and Samuel de Champlain

The answer is A, Pierre de Monts and Samuel de Champlain

21) What did they call Nova Scotia before?
    A - Arctic
    B - Metis
    C - Acadia
    D - Kanata

The answer is C, Acadia

22) When did the French and Iroquois make peace?

A - 1600
B - 1701
C - 1700
D - 1601

The answer is B, 1701

23) What drove the vast fur-trade economy of the French and Aboriginal people?

A - Demand for beaver pelts
B - Demand for squirrel pelts
C - Demand for fox furs
D - Demand for bear furs

The answer is A, Demand for beaver pelts

24) Who gave the Hudson's Bay Company exclusive rights over watershed draining in Hudson Bay?

A - Jacques Cartier
B - John Cabolt
C - King Charles II of England
D - Queen Elizabeth II

The answer is C, King Charles II of England

25) When was the trading right over watershed draining granted?

A - 1760
B - 1860

C - 1870

D - 1670

The answer is D, 1670

26) When did the English colonies along the Atlantic seaboard become richer and more populous than New France?

A - The early 1700s

B - The early 1800s

C - The early 1600s

D - The early 1500s

The answer is C, the early 1600s

27) What did they call the skilled and courageous men who traveled by canoe and formed a strong alliance with the First Nations?

A - Voyageurs and coureurs des bois

B - Paddlers and boaters

C - Settlers and immigrants

D - None of the above

The answer is A, Voyageurs and coureurs des bois

28) In what battle did the British defeat the French at Quebec City during the year of 1759?

A - Battle of the Plains of Canada

B - Battle of the Plains of Quebec

C - Battle of the Plains of Abraham

D - Battle of the British and French

The answer is C, Battle of the Plains of Abraham

29) What did Great Britain rename the colony after the war?
A - Province of Britain
B - Canada
C - Kanata
D - Province of Quebec

The answer is D, Province of Quebec

30) What did the British Parliament pass to help better govern the French Roman Catholic majority?
A - Quebec Act of 1784
B - Quebec Act of 1774
C - Quebec Act of 1874
D - Quebec Act of 1884

The answer is B, Quebec Act of 1774

31) What was formed after the 13 British colonies south of Quebec declared independence?
A - United States
B - Canada
C - Ireland
D - Asia

The answer is A, United States

32) When did the 13 colonies declare independence?

A - 1876

B - 1796

C - 1786

D - 1776

The answer is D, 1776

33) What did they call people who were loyal to the crown - who fled the oppression during the American Revolution, and settled in Nova Scotia and Quebec?

A - Settlers

B - Aboriginals

C - Loyalists

D - Villagers

The answer is C, Loyalists

34) Who led thousands of Loyalist Mohawk Indians into Canada?

A - Joseph Cartier

B - Joseph Brant

C - John Brant

D - John Cartier

The answer is B, Joseph Brant

35) Where was the first representative assembly elected?

A - Halifax, Nova Scotia in 1768

B - Toronto in 1758
C - Ottawa in 1558
D - Halifax, Nova Scotia in 1758

The answer is D, Halifax, Nova Scotia in 1758

36) What divided Quebec into Upper Canada and Lower Canada?
A - The Constitutional Act of 1781
B - The Constitutional Act of 1771
C - The Constitutional Act of 1791
D - None of the above

The answer is C, The Constitutional Act of 1791

37) Who was the first Lieutenant Governor of Upper Canada and founder of the City of York?
A - Lieutenant-Colonel John Graves Simcoe
B - Jacques Cartier
C - Count Frontenac
D - John Brant

The answer is A, Lieutenant-Colonel John Graves Simcoe

38) What was the weekly newspaper that was dedicated to anti-slavery, black immigration to Canada, temperance, and upholding British rule?
A - The Canadian Newspaper
B - The Provincial Newspaper

C - The Canadian Freeman
D - The Provincial Freeman

The answer is D, The Provincial Freeman

39) When did the British Parliament abolish the buying and selling of slaves throughout the empire?
A - 1633
B - 1733
C - 1833
D - 1933

The answer is C, 1833

40) In what year did some black Nova Scotians move on to establish Freetown, Sierra Leone (West Africa)?
A - 1878
B - 1777
C - 1792
D - 1972

The answer is C, 1792

41) What trade did the first companies of Canada compete in?
A - Mining
B - Fur trade
C - Fishing
D - Logging

The answer is B, Fur trade

42) Who ruled the waves after the defeat of Napoleon Bonaparte in the Battle of Trafalgar?

    A - The Royal Navy

    B - The Americans

    C - The Indians

    D - The Royal Marine

The answer is A, the Royal Navy

43) When was the Battle of Trafalgar?

    A - 1905

    B - 1925

    C - 1805

    D - 1825

The answer is C, 1805

44) When did the United States launch an invasion to conquer Canada?

    A - June 1912

    B - June 1812

    C - July 1812

    D - July 1812

The answer is B, June 1812

45) Who was the Major-General who captured Detroit but was killed at Queenston Heights while defending against an American attack?

    A - Lieutenant-Colonel Charles de Salaberry

B - Chief Tecumseh

C - Major-General Sir Isaac Breck

D - Major-General Sir Isaac Brock

The answer is D, Major-General Sir Isaac Brock

46) Who was the person who walked 30km to warn James FitzGibbon of an American attack?

A - Laura Secord

B - Duke of Wellington

C - Lana Secord

D - Agnes Macphail

The answer is A, Laura Secord

47) When did Upper and Lower Canada unite as the Province of Canada?

A - 1940

B - 1740

C - 1840

D - 1640

The answer is C, 1840

48) Who was the champion of French language rights that became the first head of a responsible government in Canada in 1849?

A - Sir John Alexander Macdonald

B - Sir George-Étienne Cartier

C - Sir Louis-Hippolyte La Fontaine

D - Louis Riel

The answer is C, Sir Louis-Hippolyte La Fontaine

49) What was the British North American colony who first attained full responsible government?
A - Nova Scotia
B - Ottawa
C - Quebec
D - Hudson Bay

The answer is A, Nova Scotia

50) What do you call the representatives who worked together to establish a new country?
A - Fathers of Communication
B - Fathers of Congregation
C - Fathers of Configuration
D - Fathers of Confederation

The answer is D, Fathers of Confederation

51) What are the two levels of government?
A - Federal and Provocational
B - Upper and Lower Canada
C - Federal and Provincial
D - Territorial and Provincial

The answer is C, Federal and Provincial

52) What do you call the celebration that is held every July 1st, also known as Dominion Day?

A - Manitoba Day

B - Sir John A. Macdonald Day

C - Canada Day

D - Quebec Day

The answer is C, Canada Day

53) Who suggested the term Dominion of Canada in 1864?

A - Sir Leonard Macdonald

B - Sir Leonard Tilley

C - Lord Durham

D - Sir Gregory Tilley

The answer is B, Sir Leonard Tilley

54) What inspired the term Dominion of Canada?

A - A song

B - A poem

C - Psalm 72 in the Bible

D - A quote

The answer is C, Psalm 72 in the Bible

55) Who was Canada's first Prime Minister?

A - Sir John Alexander Macdonald

B - Major-General Sir Isaac Brock

C - Sir Louis-Hippolyte La Fontaine

D - Sir George-Étienne Cartier

The answer is A, Sir John Alexander Macdonald

56) Where was the first Prime Minister of Canada born?
A - Scotland
B - Ireland
C - Greenland
D - Iceland

The answer is A, Scotland

57) Where can you find the portrait of Sir John A. Macdonald?
A - $5 bill
B - $1 bill
C - $10 bill
D - $20 bill

The answer is C, $10 bill

58) In what year did some believe that the British West Indies should become part of Canada?
A - 1870s
B - 1920s
C - 1990s
D - 1780s

The answer is B, 1920s

59) What did the first elected Assembly of Lower Canada debate on January 21, 1793?

A - Who to elect as Prime Minister

B - Whether to use both French and English

C - Whether to let women vote

D - Whether to free the slaves

The answer is B, Whether to use both French and English

60) Who seized Fort Garry from Hudson's Bay Company in 1869?

A - Prime Minister Macdonald

B - Louis Riel

C - Sir Louis-Hippolyte La Fontaine

D - Lord Durham

The answer is B, Louis Riel

61) In what year did Ottawa send soldiers to retake Fort Garry?

A - 1870

B - 1990

C - 1889

D - 1875

The answer is A, 1870

62) In what year did Prime Minister Macdonald establish the North West Mounted Police (NWMP)?

A - 1983

B - 1883

C - 1973

D - 1873

The answer is D, 1873

63) Who assigned Canada's national colors white and red in 1921?

A - King George II

B - King George V

C - Queen Elizabeth II

D - Lord Durham

The answer is B, King George V

64) Who became the first French-Canadian Prime Minister since the Confederation and encouraged immigration to the West?

A - Sir George-Étienne Cartier

B - Sir Louis-Hippolyte La Fontaine

C - Sir John Alexander Macdonald

D - Sir Wilfrid Laurier

The answer is D, Sir Wilfrid Laurier

65) What is the other term for the South African War that happened during 1899-1902?

A - Boer War

B - South War

C - Canada War

D - World War

The answer is A, Boer War

66) What did they call the nurses that served in the Royal Canadian Army Medical Corps?

A - Ladybirds

B - Blue Nurses

C - Lady Nurses

D - Bluebirds

The answer is D, Bluebirds

67) What do you call the effort by women to achieve the rights to vote?

A - Women's Voting Movement

B - Women's Suffrage Movement

C - Women's Rights Confederation

D - None of the above

The answer is B, Women's Suffrage Movement

68) Who was the first woman to serve as a Member of Parliament in 1921?

A - Laura Riel

B - Dr. Emily Stowe

C - Agnes Macphail

D - Denys Arcand

The answer is C, Agnes Macphail

69) What do you call the free association of states that the British Empire evolved into after the First World War?

A - Britain Commonwealth of Nations

B - British Commonwealth of People

C - British Commonwealth of Nations

D - Britain Commonwealth of People

The answer is C, British Commonwealth of Nations

70) What poem did Lieutenant-Colonel John McCrae compose in 1915 that is often recited on Remembrance Day?

A - In Flanders Fields

B - In Flowers Fields

C - In Flanders Garden

D - In Flowers Garden

The answer is A, In Flanders Fields

71) What led to the Great Depression or the "Dirty Thirties"?

A - Rebellion

B - Riot

C - World War II

D - Stock Market Crash

The answer is D, Stock Market Crash

72) In what years was the Bank of Canada created?

A - 1844

B - 1934

C - 1794

D - 1994

The answer is B, 1934

73) What do you call the invasion of Normandy in Northern France where Canadian troops took Juno Beach from the German Army?

A - D-Day

B - Completion Day

C - Canadian Invasion

D - None of the above

The answer is A, D-Day

74) In what year did the Second World War begin?

A - 1949

B - 1839

C - 1939

D - 1849

The answer is C, 1939

75) Who took part in the Battle of Britain for Canada?

A - Royal Canadian Navy

B - Royal Canadian Air Force

C - Marines

D - Volunteers

The answer is B, Royal Canadian Air Force

76) Who protected the convoys of ships against German submarines during the Battle of the Atlantic?

A - Royal Canadian Navy

B - Royal Canadian Air Force

C - Marines

D - Volunteers

The answer is A, Royal Canadian Navy

77) When did Japan surrender and the end four years of war in the Pacific?

A - August 24, 1975

B - August 14, 1965

C - August 24, 1955

D - August 14, 1945

The answer is D, August 14, 1945

78) What led to the relocation of Canadians of Japanese origin - and the sale of their property without compensation?

A - State of war and public opinion

B - Stock market crash

C - Rebellion

D - None of the above

The answer is A, State of war and public opinion

79) What do you call the Royal Navy frigate which led the captured USS Chesapeake into Halifax harbor?

A - HMS Charlotte

B - HMS Shannon

C - HMS Sharon

D - HMS Michael

The answer is B, HMS Shannon

80) In what year was the captured USS Chesapeake led into the Halifax Harbour?

A - 1813

B - 1887

C - 1897

D - 1883

The answer is A, 1813

Modern Canada (Answers)

1) What was discovered in Alberta in 1947 that began Canada's modern energy industry?
A - Oil
B - Electricity
C - Turbines
D - Gold

The answer is A, Oil

2) What is the meaning of the acronym GATT?
A - General Agreement on Taxes and Trades
B - General Agreement on Terrain and Trades
C - General Agreement on Tariffs and Trades
D - None of the above

The answer is C, General Agreement on Tariffs and Trades

3) In what year were the majority of Canadians able to afford adequate food and clothing for the first time?
A - 1996
B - 1967
C - 1926
D - 1951

The answer is D, 1951

4) What do you call the social assistance program that ensures common elements and a basic standard coverage?

A - Canada Health Act

B - Healthy People Act

C - Canada Welfare Act

D - Canada Insurance Act

The answer is A, Canada Health Act

5) When was Employment Insurance introduced by the federal government?

A - 1840

B - 1770

C - 1940

D - 1970

The answer is C, 1940

6) In what year was Old Age Security devised?

A - 1922

B - 1950

C - 1976

D - 1927

The answer is D, 1927

7) Who provides publicly funded education?

A - Parliament members

B - Provinces and territories

C - Volunteers

D - Churches

The answer is B, Provinces and territories

8) **What did they call the era of rapid change that Quebec experienced in the 1960s?**
A - Quiet Retaliation
B - Quiet Revolution
C - Quebec Revolution
D - Quebec Retaliation

The answer is B, Quiet Revolution

9) **In what year did the Parliament establish the Royal Commission on Bilingualism and Biculturalism?**
A - 1925
B - 1976
C - 1963
D - 1988

The answer is C, 1963

10) **This act guarantees French as well as English services by the federal government.**
A - Official Languages Act (1969)
B - Official Languages Act (1869)
C - Roaring Twenties Act (1869)
D - Official Tenties Act (1969)

The answer is A, Official Languages Act (1969)

11) **What is the international association of French-speaking countries that Canada helped found?**
A - La Anglophonie
B - French-English Association

C - French Language Association
D - La Francophonie

The answer is D, La Francophonie

12) In what year was the La Francophonie founded?
A - 1960
B - 1970
C - 1980
D - 1990

The answer is B, 1970

13) Who were the last to gain the right to vote in 1948?
A - Japanese-English
B - Japanese-Canadians
C - British-Canadian
D - Japanese-British

The answer is B, Japanese-Canadians

14) In what year did the Communist victory in the Vietnam war lead to many Vietnamese fleeing and searching for refuge in Canada?
A - 1975
B - 1985
C - 1889
D - 1995

The answer is A, 1975

15) What was founded in 1920 when a style of painting captured the rugged wilderness?

A - Team of Seven

B - Group with Seven

C - Team with Seven

D - Group of Seven

The answer is D, Group of Seven

16) Who pioneered modern Inuit art with etchings, prints, and soapstone sculptures?

A - Denys Arcand

B - Louis-Philippe Hébert

C - Norman Jewison

D - Atom Egoyan

The answer is B, Louis-Philippe Hébert

17) What sport did the Canadian James Naismith invent in 1891?

A - Basketball

B - Tennis

C - Hockey

D - Football

The answer is A, Basketball

18) Who became the world record sprinter and double Olympic gold medalist in 1996 at the Olympic Summer Games?

A - Denys Arcand

B - Wayne Gretzky
C - Marshall McLuhan
D - Donovan Bailey

The answer is D, Donovan Bailey

19) What did they call the cross-country run that Terry Fox started in 1980 to raise money for cancer research?
A - Marathon of Faith
B - Marathon of Hope
C - Run of Hope
D - Run of Faith

The answer is B, Marathon of Hope

20) In what year did the British Columbian Rick Hansen circle the globe to raise funds for spinal cord research?
A - 1985
B - 1885
C - 1785
D - 1685

The answer is A, 1985

21) What did Sir Frederick Banting and Charles Best discover to treat diabetes?
A - Antibiotic
B - Penicillin
C - Booster
D - Insulin

The answer is D, Insulin

22) In what year did Paul Henderson score the important goal for Canada in the Canada-Soviet Summit Series, often referred to as "the goal heard around the world"?
A - 1872
B - 1772
C - 1972
D - 1982

The answer is C, 1972

23) What does the acronym NATO stand for?
A - North Atlantic Team Organization
B - North Atlantic Treaty Organization
C - North Arctic Treaty Organization
D - North Acadia Treaty Organization

The answer is B, North Atlantic Treaty Organization

24) Who is the Olympic gold medalist and prominent activist for gay and lesbian Canadians?
A - Edmonton Oilers
B - Chantal Peticlerc
C - Mark Tewksbury
D - Rick Hansen

The answer is C, Mark Tewksbury

25) In which team did Wayne Gretzky play from 1978-1988?
A - Edmonton Oilers

B - Boston Bruins

C - Montreal Canadiens

D - Calgary Flames

The answer is A, Edmonton Oilers

26) In what year were the Aboriginal people granted the right to vote?

A - 1660

B - 1760

C - 1860

D - 1960

The answer is D, 1960

27) In what year did the Canadian Space Agency and Canadian astronauts participate in space exploration, using the Canadian-designed and built Canadarm?

A - 1889

B - 1989

C - 1879

D - 1979

The answer is B, 1989

28) What did Joseph-Armand Bombardier invent?

A - The Snowmobile

B - The Light Bulb

C - Insulin

D - The Telephone

The answer is A, the Snowmobile

29) What did Matthew Evans and Henry Woodward invent?

A - Telephone

B - Electric light bulb

C - Insulin

D - Electric car

The answer is B, the Electric Light Bulb

30) Who invented the first cardiac pacemaker?

A - Dr. Wilder Penfield

B - Sir Sanford Flemming

C - Jim Balsillie

D - Dr. John A. Hopps

The answer is D, Dr. John A. Hopps

How Canadians Govern Themselves (Answers)

1) How many governments are there in Canada?
A - Three
B - One
C - Four
D - Two

The answer is C, Four

2) What do you call a government that takes responsibility for matters of both national and international concern?
A - Federal State
B - National State
C - Municipal
D - Judicial

The answer is A, Federal State

3) Which of the following is not in the scope of the Federal State?
A - Foreign Policy
B - Interprovincial Trade and Communications
C - Criminal Law and Citizenship
D - None of the above

The answer is D, None of the above

4) **Which of the following is not part of the responsibility of the Provincial government?**

A - Education

B - Defence

C - Health

D - Municipal Government

The answer is B, Defence

5) **The federal government and the provinces share what jurisdiction?**

A - Agriculture and Defence

B - Agriculture and Immigration

C - Education and Defence

D - Immigration and Health

The answer is B, Agriculture and Immigration

6) **Which of these allows provinces to form policies for their own populations?**

A - State

B - Democratic

C - Federalism

D - Provincial

The answer is C, Federalism

7) **What do you call the system in which members are elected to the House of Commons in Ottawa - by the people?**

A - Federalism

B - Sovereignty

C - Parliamentary Democracy

D - Federal Democracy

The answer is C, Parliamentary Democracy

8) **Which of the following is not part of the responsibility of the representatives?**

A - Approving and monitoring expenditures

B - Keeping the government accountable

C - Passing of laws

D - None of the above

The answer is D, None of the above

9) **Who is responsible to the elected representatives?**

A - Cabinet ministers

B - Sovereign

C - Prime Minister

D - Assembly members

The answer is A, Cabinet ministers

10) **The Parliament has how many parts?**

A - Three

B - Four

C - Five

D - One

The answer is A, Three

11) **Which of the following is not part of the Parliament?**

A - House of Commons

B - Senate

C - Municipal

D - Sovereign

The answer is C, Municipal

12) **Who is responsible in selecting Cabinet members as well as responsible for the operations and policy of the government?**

A - President

B - Prime Minister

C - King

D - House Speaker

The answer is B, Prime Minister

13) **What do you call the chamber elected by the people every four years?**

A - Member of the jury

B - Cabinet members

C - House of Representative

D - House of Commons

The answer is D, House of Commons

14) **Who appoints the Senators on the advice of the Prime Minister?**

A - The King

B - Representatives

C - The Governor General

D - Cabinet Ministers

The answer is C, the Governor General

15) Until what age can the Senators stay in position?

A - 75 years old

B - 85 years old

C - 100 years old

D - 65 years old

The answer is A, 75 years old

16) What do you call the proposal for new laws that both the House of Commons and Senate consider and review?

A - Laws

B - Legislative

C - Proposals

D - Bills

The answer is D, Bills

17) What does the Governor General grant on behalf of the sovereign before passing a bill to become a law?

A - Royal seal

B - Royal assent

C - Medal

D - Signature

The answer is B, Royal assent

18) How many steps are there in making a law?
   A - Four
   B - Five
   C - Six
   D - Seven

The answer is D, Seven

19) What is the 5th step in the legislative process of making a new law?
   A - The members debate and vote on the bill
   B - Members can make other amendments
   C - Members debate the bill's principle
   D - Committee members study the bill clause by clause

The answer is A, The members debate and vote on the bill.

20) What happens in the 2nd step in the legislative process of making a new law?
   A - Committee members study the bill clause by clause
   B - The members debate the bills principle
   C - The bill follows a similar process in the senate
   D - Members debate and vote on the bill

The answer is B, The members debate the bills principle.

21) At what age can Canadian citizens vote?

    A - 16 years old

    B- 17 years old

    C - 19 years old

    D - 18 years old

The answer is D, 18 years old

22) Who represents the sovereign in the 10 provinces?

    A - Governor General

    B - Prime Minister

    C - Lieutenant Governor

    D - Cabinet members

The answer is C, Lieutenant Governor

23) Who appoints the Lieutenant Governor on the advice of the Prime Minister?

    A - Governor General

    B - Lieutenant Governor

    C - Prime Minister

    D - King

The answer is A, Governor General

24) Who is the 28th Governor General since the Confederation?

    A - David Jonstone

    B - David Jonson

    C - David Hudson

    D - David Johnston

The answer is D, David Johnston

25) In the three territories, who represents the federal government and plays a ceremonial role?

A - Cabinet members

B - Commissioner

C - Speaker

D - Governor General

The answer is B, Commissioner

26) Which are not members of the legislature?

A - Members of the Legislative Assembly

B - Members of the Provincial Parliament

C - Members of the National Association

D - Members of the House of Assembly

The answer is C, Members of the National Association

27) In each province, who has a similar role to the Prime Minister in the federal government?

A - Premier

B - Lieutenant General

C - Commissioner

D - Head of State

The answer is A, Premier

28) Which of the following is not included in the three branches of government?

A - Legislative

B - Judicial

C - Executive

D - Federal

The answer is D, Federal

29) Complete these three key facts about Canada's system of government: Canada is a federal state, a parliamentary democracy, and a _____ monarchy.

A - Constitutional

B - Provincial

C - Institutional

D - Federal

The answer is A, Constitutional

30) In what Act were the responsibilities of the federal and provincial government defined?

A - Constitution Act, 1967

B - Constitution Act, 1867

C - Constitution Act, 1987

D - Constitution Act, 1897

The answer is B, Constitution Act, 1867

Federal Elections (Answers)

1) When is the federal election held under legislation passed by Parliament?

A - Second Monday in October, every four years

B - Third Monday in October, every four years

C - Second Monday in November, every four years

D - Third Monday in November, every four years

The answer is B, Third Monday in October, every four years

2) What do you call the geographical area represented by a member of Parliament (MP)?

A - Electoral District

B - Sovereign

C - Electoral Post

D - Voting District

The answer is A, Electoral District

3) Canada is divided into how many electoral districts?

A - 508

B - 448

C - 318

D - 308

The answer is D, 308

4) What do you call people who run for office?

A - Members

B - Candidates

C - Solicitors

D - Officials

The answer is B, Candidates

5) Which of the following shows that you are eligible to vote?

A - Being a Canadian Citizen

B - Being on the voter's list

C - Being at least 18 years old on voting day

D - All of the above

The answer is D, All of the above

6) Who produces the voters' lists used during federal elections and referendums?

A - Cabinet members

B - Electors Committee

C - Elections Canada

D - None of the above

The answer is C, Elections Canada

7) What do Elections Canada mail to each person whose name is found in the National Register of Electors?

A - Voter Information Card

B - Ballots

179

C - Lists of candidates
D - Guide in voting

The answer is A, Voter Information Card

8) **Which Canadian law ensures that nobody can watch you vote?**
A - the right to vote freely
B - the right to skip vote
C - the right to a secret ballot
D - None of the above

The answer is C, the right to a secret ballot

9) **What do you call the party in power that holds over 50% of seats in the House of Commons?**
A - Minority government
B - Majority government
C - Minority committee
D - Majority committee

The answer is B, Majority government

10) **What do you call the party that holds less than 50% of the seats in the House of Commons?**
A - Majority committee
B - Minority committee
C - Majority government
D - Minority government

The answer is D, Minority government

11) Who chooses the ministers of the Crown from members of the House of Commons?

A - Secretary

B - Lieutenant General

C - Governor General

D - Prime Minister

The answer is D, Prime Minister

12) Who are responsible for running the federal government departments?

A - Cabinet Ministers

B - King

C - Prime Minister

D - Governor General

The answer is A, Cabinet Ministers

13) What do you call the Cabinet ministers and the Prime Minister?

A - Members

B - Parliaments

C - Cabinet

D - Commoners

The answer is C, Cabinet

14) What do you call the party that peacefully opposes or tries to improve government proposals?

A - House of Opposition

B - Opposition Parties

C - Opposition Committee

D - None of the above

The answer is B, Opposition Parties

15) Which of the following is not included in the current three major political parties represented in the House of Commons?

A - Conservative

B - Liberal

C - Federal

D - New Democratic

The answer is C, Federal

16) How many procedures are there in voting?

A - Five

B - Six

C - Seven

D - Eight

The answer is D, Eight

17) What should you do if you don't get a voter information card?

A - Call your local elections office

B - Skip and vote in the next election

C - Use a family's voter information card

D - None of the above

The answer is A, Call your local elections office

18) When voting, how do you mark the name of the candidate of your choice?

A - Shade the circle next to the candidate.

B - Put an "X" in the circle next to the candidates name.

C - Cross out the name of the candidate

D - Underline the name of the candidate

The answer is B, Put an "X" in the circle of the candidates name.

19) Who will be the one to tear off the ballot number after you have finished voting?

A - You

B - Police

C - Poll Official

D - Ballot numbers should not be teared off

The answer is C, Poll Official

20) Where do you deposit your ballot after voting?

A - At home

B - In the ballot box

C - Give it to the poll official

D - Throw it in the trash

The answer is B, Ballot box

21) What do you call laws that the Municipal government passes which only affects the local community?

A - Bill

B - By-laws

C - Laws

D - Proposals

The answer is B, By-laws

22) What is the other term for mayor which councils usually include in the municipal government?

A - Lieutenant-Governor

B - Cabinet

C - Chief

D - Revee

The answer is D, Revee

23) What is the other term for councilors which councils usually include in the municipal government?

A - Eldermen

B - Aldermen

C - Chief

D - Revee

The answer is B, Aldermen

24) Which of the following is part of the responsibility of municipalities?

A - Snow removal

B - Public transit

C - Urban or regional planning

D - All of the above

The answer is D, All of the above

25) Which of the following is not part of the responsibility of the Members of the Legislative Assembly?

A - Highways

B - Education

C - Recycling Programs

D - Property and Civil Rights

The answer is C, Recycling Programs

26) The following are shared responsibilities of both Members of Parliament and the Members of the Legislative Assembly, except for one, which is it?

A - Criminal Justice

B - Agriculture

C - Environment

D - Immigration

The answer is A, Criminal Justice

27) Who are the ones elected during the Provincial and Territorial Election?

A - Members of the House of Assembly

B - Members of the Provincial Parliament

C - Members of the National Association

D - Members of the Legislative Assembly

The answer is C, Members of the National Association

28) Who are the ones elected during the Federal Elections?

A - Prime Minister

B - Members of Parliament

C - Cabinet Members

D - Governor-General

The answer is B, Members of Parliament

29) Who are the ones elected during the Municipal Elections?

A - Mayor and Councilors

B - Mayor and Reeve

C - Councilors and Aldermen

D - None of the Above

The answer is A, Mayor and Councilors

30) Which of the following is not part of the responsibility of the Members of Parliament?

A - Aboriginal Affairs

B - National Defence

C - Social and Community Health

D - International Trade

The answer is C, Social and Community Health

The Justice System (Answers)

1) This guarantees everyone due process under the law.
A - Bills
B - Canadian Justice System
C - Rights
D - Judge

The answer is B, Canadian Justice System

2) What is meant by the term "Presumption of Innocence"?
A - Everyone is innocent until proven guilty
B - Everyone is not innocent until proven guilty
C - Everyone is guilty until proven innocent
D - None of the above

The answer is A, everyone is innocent until proven guilty

3) This principle states that the government must respect all legal rights each person is entitled to under the law.
A - Rule of Law
B - Democratic Principles
C - Due Process
D - Freedom under the law

The answer is C, Due Process

4) **What symbolizes the impartial manner of our laws - blind to all considerations but all facts?**
   A - Blindfolded Lady Justice
   B - Scale
   C - Hammer
   D - Statue of Liberty

The answer is A, Blindfolded Lady Justice

5) **These are intended to provide order in society, and to express the values/beliefs of Canadians.**
   A - Bills
   B - Rights
   C - Laws
   D - Proposal

The answer is C, Laws

6) **What do you call Canada's highest court?**
   A - House of Commons
   B - Supreme Court of Canada
   C - Trial Court
   D - Federal Court of Canada

The answer is B, Supreme Court of Canada

7) **Which court deals with matters concerning the federal government?**
   A - House of Commons
   B - Supreme Court of Canada

C - Trial Court

D - Federal Court of Canada

The answer is D, Federal Court of Canada

8) **The following courts deal with civil cases involving small sums of money. Which of the following is not accurate?**
   A - Federal Court of Canada
   B - Traffic Court
   C - Family Court
   D - Small Claims Court

The answer is A, Federal Court of Canada

9) **Who keeps the people safe and enforces the law?**
   A - Councilors
   B - Members of Parliament
   C - Mayor
   D - Police

The answer is D, Police

10) **What do you call the police forces that are present in Ontario and Quebec?**
   A - Members of the Police Force
   B - Provincial Police Forces
   C - Quebec Police Force
   D - Ontario Police Force

The answer is B, Provincial Police Forces

11) What do you call the police force who enforces federal laws throughout Canada?

A - Royal Canadian Member Police

B - Royal Canadian Mounted Police

C - Royal Captain Member Police

D - Royal Captain Mounted Police

The answer is B, Royal Canadian Mounted Police

12) Who can help you with legal problems and act for you in court?

A - Lawyers

B - Police

C - Jury

D - Witness

The answer is A, Lawyers

13) This place has an essential role in punishing criminals and deterring crime.

A - House

B - Crime Scene

C - Prisons

D - Parliament

The answer is C, Prisons

14) What is another term for Trial Court?

A - Court of Municipal

B - Provincial court

C - Court of Commons

D - Court of Queen's Bench

The answer is D, Court of Queen's Bench

15) In what situations can you ask the police for help?

A - If there's been an accident

B - If you lost something

C - If you see a crime taking place

D - All of the above

The answer is D, All of the above

Canadian Symbols (Answers)

1) What has been the symbol of Canada for 400 years? This is a symbol of government, including the parliament, the legislature, the courts, police services, and the Canadian Forces?

A - Maple leaf

B - Crown

C - Pen

D - Lady Justice

The answer is B, Crown

2) In what year was the new Canadian flag raised?

A - 1965

B - 1865

C - 1995

D - 1975

The answer is A, 1965

3) Where did the red-white-red pattern of the flag come from?

A - From the flag of the British Royal Army

B - Proposed by the House of Commons

C - From the flag of the Royal Military College

D - None of the above

The answer is C, from the Royal Military College flag.

4) **What do you call the official Royal Flag?**
   A - Unified Jack
   B - Union Flag
   C - Unified Nation
   D - Union Jack

The answer is D, Union Jack

5) **What is Canada's best-known symbol that was adopted by French Canadians in the 1700s and carved in the headstones of the fallen soldiers?**
   A - Crown
   B - Lady Justice
   C - Maple Leaf
   D - Pen

The answer is C, Maple Leaf

6) **What do you call the symbol that was adopted by the French king in 496? It also became a symbol of French royalty?**
   A - Maple Leaf
   B - Lily Flower
   C - Lily of the Valley
   D - Rose

The answer is B, Lily Flower

7) **What is another name for Lily Flower which was used as the symbol of French royalty?**
   A - Fleur-de-lys
   B - Flower of French

C - Royal Flower

D - None of the above

The answer is A, fleur-de-lys

8) **What is the coat of arms and national motto that Canada adopted after the First World War?**

A - National Pride of Canadians

B - To you from failing hands we throw

C - We lived, felt dawn, saw sunset glow

D - A mari usque ad mare

The answer is D, A mari usque ad mare

9) **What does the coat of arms and national motto mean?**

A - From land to land

B - From land to sea

C - From sea to sea

D - From land to shining sea

The answer is C, From sea to sea

10) **Which of the following is not included in the Parliament Buildings that embody the French, English, and Aboriginal traditions?**

A - Stained glass

B - Arches

C - Sculptures

D - Scale

The answer is D, Scale

11) When were the parliament buildings completed?

A -1950s

B - 1960s

C - 1970s

D - 1980s

The answer is B, 1960s

12) What destroyed the Centre Block in 1916?

A - Accidental fire

B - Arson

C - Riot

D - Earthquake

The answer is A, Accidental fire

13) In what year was the Centre Block rebuilt?

A - 1722

B - 1827

C - 1977

D - 1922

The answer is D, 1922

14) What was built in 1927 to remember the First World War?

A - Statue of Liberty

B - The Peace Tower

C - Parliament Buildings

D - Eiffel Tower

The answer is B, The Peace Tower

15) What do you call the books in the Memorial Chamber that holds soldiers, sailors, and airmen's names - of those who died serving Canada in war/on duty?
A - Obituary
B - Book of the Dead
C - Books of Remembrance
D - Book of Memorial

The answer is C, Books of Remembrance

16) The following architectural styles are used in the legislature of the other provinces. Which of the following is not included?
A - Baroque
B - French Second Empire Style
C - Neoclassical
D - Romanesque

The answer is B, French Second Empire Style

17) What is Canada's most popular spectator sport and is considered the national winter sport?
A - Polo
B - Basketball
C - Ice Skating
D - Hockey

The answer is D, Hockey

18) When was Ice Hockey developed in Canada?

A - 1600s

B - 1700s

C - 1800s

D - 1900s

The answer is C, 1800s

19) What is the name of the item that Lord Stanley donated in 1892 that the National Hockey League plays for?

A - Stanley Cup

B - Hockey Cup

C - Stanley Trophy

D - Hockey Trophy

The answer is A, Stanley Cup

20) What is the name of the cup that is awarded for women's hockey?

A - Women's Cup

B - Hockey Cup

C - Stanley Cup

D - Clarkson Cup

The answer is D, Clarkson Cup

21) What is the 2nd most popular sport in Canada?

A - Basketball

B - Canadian Football

C - Polo

D - Lacrosse

The answer is B, Canadian Football

22) What do you call the ice game introduced by Scottish pioneers?

A - Curling

B - Figure Ice Skating

C - Sledding

D - Skiing

The answer is A, Curling

23) What do you call the official summer sport that was first played by the Aboriginals?

A - Polo

B - Lacrosse

C - Swimming

D - Acrobats

The answer is B, Lacrosse

24) What was adopted as a symbol of Hudson's Bay Company?

A - Hummingbird

B - Beaver

C - Koala

D - Raccoon

The answer is B. Beaver

25) What French-Canadian patriotic association used the beaver as an emblem in 1834?

A - St. Jean Baptiste Society

B - St. Paul Society

C - St. Evangeline Society

D - St. Michael Society

The answer is A, St. Jean Baptiste Society

26) At what age are applicants exempted from needing adequate knowledge in English or French to become a Canadian Citizen?

A - 45 years old

B - 55 years old

C - 65 years old

D - 75 years old

The answer is B, 55 years old

27) What is Canada's national anthem?

A - Hail Canada

B - Beloved Canada

C - Lovely Canada

D - O Canada

The answer is D, O Canada

28) In what year was Canada's national anthem proclaimed?

A - 1870

B - 1980

C - 1990

D - 1890

The answer is B, 1980

29) Where was the national anthem first sung?
A - Quebec City

B - Toronto

C - Vancouver

D - Ottawa

The answer is A, Quebec City

30) What is the title of the Royal Anthem of Canada?
A - Royal Canada

B - God Save the King

C - O Canada

D - Beloved Canada

The answer is B, God Save the King

31) What did the jazz pianist Oscar Peterson receive from Roland Michener in 1973?
A - Order of Court

B - Medal of Valor

C - Victoria Cross

D - Order of Canada

The answer is D, Order of Canada

32) What do official awards or honors consist of?
A - Orders

B - Decorations
C - Medals
D - All of the above

The answer is D, All of the above

33) When was Canada's own honor system, the Order of Canada, started?
A - 1947
B - 1957
C - 1967
D - 1977

The answer is C, 1967

34) What do you call the highest honor available to Canadians?
A - Medal of Valor
B - Victoria Cross
C - Order of Canada
D - Medal of Honor

The answer is B, Victoria Cross

35) How many Canadians have been awarded the Victoria Cross, since 1854?
A - 66
B - 76
C - 86
D - 96

The answer is D, 96 Canadians.

36) Who was the first Canadian to be awarded the Victoria Cross?

A - Corporal Filip Konowal

B - Lieutenant Robert Hampton Gray

C - Lieutenant Alexander Roberts Dunn

D - Captain Paul Triquet

The answer is C, Lieutenant Alexander Roberts Dunn

37) Who was the first black male to be given the Victoria Cross?

A - Able Seaman William Hall

B - Lieutenant Robert Hampton Gray

C - Captain Paul Triquet

D - Lieutenant Alexander Roberts Dunn

The answer is A, Able Seaman William Hall

38) Who was the flying ace that received the Victoria Cross during the First World War?

A - Lieutenant Alexander Roberts Dunn

B - Able Seaman William Hall

C - Captain Paul Triquet

D - Captain Billy Bishop

The answer is D, Captain Billy Bishop

39) Who was the first member of the Canadian Corps not born inside the British Empire to be given the VC?

A - Captain Paul Triquet

B - Corporal Filip Konowal

C - Lieutenant Alexander Roberts Dunn

D - Able Seaman William Hall

The answer is B, Corporal Filip Konowal

40) When is Sir Wilfrid Laurier Day celebrated?

A - December 20

B - November 20

C - November 12

D - August 11

The answer is B, November 20

THE CANADIAN CITIZENSHIP TEST

Canada's Economy (Answers)

1) **When did Canada enact free trade with the United States?**
   A - 1968
   B - 1978
   C - 1988
   D - 1998

The answer is C, 1988

2) **What does NAFTA stand for?**
   A - North American Free Trade Agreement
   B - North American Free Trade Associated
   C - North Acadia Free Trade Agreement
   D - North American Free Train Agreement

The answer is A, North American Free Trade Agreement

3) **Which of the following is included in the three main types of Canada's industries?**
   A - Natural resources industries
   B - Service industries
   C - Manufacturing industries
   D - All of the above

The answer is D, All of the above

4) **What % of Canadians now work in service industries?**
   A - 65%
   B - 75%

C - 85%

D - 95%

The answer is B, 75%

5) **Which of the following is not included in the Service industries?**

A - Health care

B - Education

C - Transportation

D - Energy

The answer is D, Energy

6) **Who is Canada's largest international trading partner?**

A - United States

B - Britain

C - Australia

D - China

The answer is A, United States

7) **What do you call the border that Canadians and Americans cross every year in safety?**

A - The world's longest undivided border

B - The world's longest undefended border

C - The world's longest unified border

D - The world's safest undefended border

The answer is B, The world's longest undefended border

8) Where can you find the words "children of common mother" inscribed?

A - Parliament Building

B - Statue of Liberty

C - Courts

D - Peace Arch

The answer is D, Peace Arch

9) What does the Peace Arch symbolize?

A - Close ties and common interest

B - Freedom

C - Trade partner

D - None of the above

The answer is A, Close ties and common interest

10) Where is the Peace Arch located?

A - Blaine in the State of Texas

B - Blaine in the State of Washington

C - Blaine in the State of Ohio

D - Blaine in the State of Illinois

The answer is B, Blaine in the State of Washington

11) What is the estimated Canadian export destined for the U.S.A?

A - Three-quarters

B - Two-thirds

C - Half

D - One-quarter

The answer is A, Three-quarters

12) What remains as the engine of Canada's economic growth?

A - Mining

B - Fishery

C - Logging

D - Commerce

The answer is D, Commerce

13) Which country became a partner in 1994 as part of the broader North American Free Trade Agreement (NAFTA)?

A - Paris

B - Mexico

C - Russia

D - Japan

The answer is B, Mexico

14) What type of dam can be found in Saguenay River, Quebec?

A - Hydro-Electric Dam

B - Diversion Dam

C - Coffer Dam

D - Industrial Waste Dam

The answer is A, Hydro-Electric Dam

15) Which industry makes products to sell in Canada and around the world?

A - Service

B - Manufacturing

C - Shipping

D - Natural resources

The answer is B, Manufacturing

16) Which of the following is included in the manufactured products that Canada sells?

A - Automobiles

B - Paper

C - Aerospace technology

D - All of the above

The answer is D, All of the above

Canada's Regions (Answers)

1) What is Canada known as?

   A - 3rd largest country on earth

   B - 4th largest country on earth

   C - 2nd largest country on earth

   D - 5th largest country on earth

The answer is C, 2nd largest country on earth

2) How many oceans line Canada's frontier?

   A - 2

   B - 3

   C - 4

   D - 5

The answer is B, 3

3) What is the ocean that lines Canada's frontier to the east?

   A - Indian

   B - Pacific

   C - Atlantic

   D - Arctic

The answer is C, Atlantic

4) What is the ocean that lines Canada's frontier to the north?

   A - Atlantic

   B - Indian

   C - Pacific

   D - Arctic

The answer is D, Arctic

5) What is the ocean that lines Canada's frontier to the west?

A - Arctic

B - Pacific

C - Indian

D - Atlantic

The answer is B, Pacific

6) How many regions does Canada have?

A - 5

B - 6

C - 7

D - 8

The answer is A, 5

7) Which of the following is part of Canada's Regions?

A - Central Canada

B - The West Coast

C - The Northern Territories

D - All of the above

The answer is D, All of the above

8) In what year was Ottawa chosen as the capital?

A - 1997

B - 1857

C - 1700

D - 1888

The answer is B, 1857

9) **What is Canada's fourth largest metropolitan area?**
   A - Vancouver
   B - Toronto
   C - Ottawa
   D - New Brunswick

The answer is C, Ottawa

10) **Who decided on Ottawa as the capital in 1857?**
   A - Queen Victoria
   B - Frederic
   C - Nunavut
   D - Ontario

The answer is A, Queen Victoria

11) **How many square kilometers is the National Capital Region surrounding Ottawa?**
   A - 4,500 square kilometers
   B - 3,700 square kilometers
   C - 5,000 square kilometers
   D - 4,700 square kilometers

The answer is D, 4,700 square kilometers

12) **How many Provinces does Canada have?**
   A - 11
   B - 9
   C - 10
   D - 15

The answer is C, 10

13) How many territories does Canada have?

A - 3

B - 4

C - 5

D - 6

The answer is A, 3

14) What do each province and territory in Canada have?

A - Court

B - Parliament

C - Land measurement

D - Capital City

The answer is D, Capital City

15) What is the estimated count of Canada's population?

A - 44 million

B - 34 million

C - 15 million

D - 47 million

The answer is B, 34 million

16) What is the name of a now tourist attraction and winter skateway that was once a military waterway?

A - Ottawa's Great Canal

B - Ontario's Rideau Canal

C - Ottawa's Rideau Canal

D - Ontario's Great Canal

The answer is C, Ottawa's Rideau Canal

17) What is the Capital City of Ontario Province?
A - Ottawa
B - Vancouver
C - Toronto
D - Quebec

The answer is C, Toronto

18) Which of the following is not part of Prairie Provinces?
A - Saskatchewan
B - British Columbia
C - Alberta
D - Manitoba

The answer is B, British Columbia

19) What is the Capital City of British Columbia?
A - Victoria
B - Charlottetown
C - Fredericton
D - Winnipeg

The answer is A, Victoria

20) Which of the following is not included in Atlantic Provinces?
A - British Columbia
B - Manitoba
C - Nunavut
D - All of the above

The answer is D, All of the above

21) What is New Brunswick's Capital City?
A - Winnipeg
B - Fredericton
C - Nunavut
D - Alberta

The answer is B, Fredericton

22) What is Prince Edward Island's Capital City?
A - Alberta
B - Fredericton
C - Winnipeg
D - Charlottetown

The answer is D, Charlottetown

23) St. John's is the capital city of what province?
A - Nova Scotia
B - New Brunswick
C - Newfoundland and Labrador
D - Quebec

The answer is C, Newfoundland and Labrador

24) Fredericton is the capital city of what province?
A - Quebec
B - New Brunswick
C - Nova Scotia
D - Nunavut

The answer is B, New Brunswick

25) Regina is the capital city of what province?

A - Saskatchewan

B - Nova Scotia

C - Nunavut

D - Alberta

The answer is A, Saskatchewan

26) Manitoba is part of what province?

A - Atlantic Provinces

B - West Coast

C - Prairie provinces

D - Central Canada

The answer is C, Prairie provinces

27) Nova Scotia is part of what province?

A - Central Canada

B - West Coast

C - Prairie provinces

D - Atlantic provinces

The answer is D, Atlantic provinces

28) Which of the following is not Canada's territory?

A - Northwest Territories

B - Southwest Territories

C - Yukon Territory

D - Nunavut

The answer is B, Southwest Territories

215

29) Where is the most easterly point in Northern America that has its own time zone?

A - Newfoundland and Labrador

B - British Columbia

C - Nunavut

D - Prince Edward Island

The answer is A, Newfoundland and Labrador

30) What is the smallest province that is known for its beaches, red soil, and agriculture, especially potatoes?

A - British Columbia

B - Saskatchewan

C - Manitoba

D - Prince Edward Island

The answer is D, Prince Edward Island

31) What does the province of Labrador have immensely?

A - Ship manufacturing

B - Hydro-electric resources

C - Fishery

D - Mining

The answer is B, Hydro-electric resources

32) What do you call the bridge that connects Prince Edward Island to mainland Canada?

A - San Juanico Bridge

B - Golden Gate Bridge

C - Confederation Bridge

D - Canada Bridge

The answer is C, Confederation Bridge

33) What is the title of the fable about the happenings of a red-headed orphan girl by Lucy Maud Montgomery that was set in Prince Edward Island?

A - Anna Banana

B - Anne of Green Gables

C - Princess Sarah

D - Princess Diaries

The answer is B, Anne of Green Gables

34) What is the most populated Atlantic Province and a gateway to Canada?

A - Nova Scotia

B - Alberta

C - Saskatchewan

D - Manitoba

The answer is A, Nova Scotia

35) What is Nova Scotia's Capital City?

A - Winnipeg

B - Alberta

C - Halifax

D - Edmonton

The answer is C, Halifax

36) The following are part of Nova Scotia's identity except for one, which is it?

A - Mining

B - Fisheries

C - Shipbuilding

D - Shipping

The answer is A, Mining

37) What tradition sustains a vibrant culture in Nova Scotia?

A - French tradition

B - Aboriginal traditional

C - Celtic and Gaelic tradition

D - Irish tradition

The answer is C, Celtic and Gaelic tradition

38) What is Halifax home to?

A - Fishery

B - Coal mining

C - Ship building

D - Canada's largest naval base

The answer is D, Canada's largest naval base

39) How many annual festivals does Nova Scotia hold?

A - Over 800

B - Over 500

C - Over 700

D - Over 600

The answer is C, over 700

40) What is the province that was founded by United Empire Loyalists and also has the 2nd largest river system on North America's Atlantic coastline?

A - Manitoba

B - Nunavut

C - New Brunswick

D - Alberta

The answer is C, New Brunswick

41) What do you call the 2nd biggest river system on North America's Atlantic coastline?

A - St. John River system

B - North America River system

C - Canada River system

D - Atlantic River system

The answer is A, St. John River system

42) Which of the following is New Brunswick's principal industry?

A - Agriculture

B - Forestry

C - Mining

D - All of the above

The answer is D, All of the above

43) What is New Brunswick's principal Francophone Acadian center?
A - Vancouver
B - Ottawa
C - Moncton
D - Manitoba

The answer is C, Moncton

44) What is New Brunswick's largest city, port, and manufacturing center?
A - Manitoba
B - Saint John
C - Moncton
D - Vancouver

The answer is B, Saint John

45) What do you call the area near the Great Lakes/St. Lawrence River in southern Quebec and Ontario?
A - Main Canada
B - Great Lakes Canada
C - St. John River
D - Central Canada

The answer is D, Central Canada

46) Which provinces produce more than 3/4 of all Canadian manufactured goods?
A - Ontario and Manitoba
B - Ontario and Quebec

C - Quebec and Alberta

D - Quebec and Regina

The answer is B, Ontario and Quebec

47) What kind of winters and summers do Ontario and Quebec have?

A - Cold winters and warm humid summer

B - Harsh winter and dry summer

C - Mild winter and humid summer

D - Cold winter and cool summer

The answer is A, Cold winters, and warm humid summer

48) Which province is Canada's main producer of pulp and paper?

A - Ontario

B - Manitoba

C - Regina

D - Quebec

The answer is D, Quebec

49) What is Quebec known for, having a huge supply of fresh water?

A - Canada's largest producer of naval ships

B - Canada's largest producer of hydroelectricity

C - Canada's largest fishery

D - Canada's largest producer of dams

The answer is B, Canada's largest producer of hydroelectricity

50) What is Canada's 2nd largest city and the 2nd largest French-speaking city in the world behind Paris?

A - Manitoba

B - Regina

C - Montreal

D - Edmonton

The answer is C, Montreal

51) What is the largest city in Canada and also the country's main financial center?

A - Vancouver

B - Montreal

C - Halifax

D - Toronto

The answer is D, Toronto

52) What is known for its vineyards, wines, waterfall, and fruit crops?

A - Halifax

B - Yukon Territory

C - Alberta

D - Niagara Region

The answer is D, Niagara Region

53) Which of the following do Ontario farmers raise?

A - Poultry

B - Dairy and beef cattle

C - Vegetable and grain crops

D - All of the above

The answer is D, All of the above

54) How many lakes are there located between Ontario and the United States?

A - 4

B - 5

C - 6

D - 7

The answer is B, 5

55) Which of these is the largest freshwater lake in the world?

A - Lake Superior

B - Grand Lake

C - Lake Erie

D - Lake Huron

The answer is A, Lake Superior

56) What is the name of the province whose economy relies on agriculture, mining, and hydro-electric generation, with Winnipeg as the most populated city?

A - Ottawa

B - Saskatchewan

C - Ontario

D - Manitoba

The answer is D, Manitoba

57) **What is the most famous street intersection in Canada?**
A - Montage and Main
B - Portage and Main
C - Fountain and Main
D - Porridge and Main

The answer is B, Portage and Main

58) **What do you call Winnipeg's French Quarter that has Western Canada's largest Francophone community?**
A - St. John's
B - St. Paul
C - St. Boniface
D - St. Andrew's

The answer is C, St. Boniface

59) **What is the estimated percentage of people with Ukrainian origins living in Manitoba?**
A - 14%
B - 15%
C - 16%
D - 17%

The answer is A, 14%

60) **What is the estimated percentage of Aboriginal populations living in Manitoba?**
A - 14%
B - 15%

C - 16%

D - 17%

The answer is B, 15%

61) The province of Saskatchewan was known as what?

A - Bed and breakfast of the world

B - Breadbasket of the world

C - Rice province

D - None of the above

The answer is B, Breadbasket of the world

62) Saskatchewan is the country's largest producer of what?

A - Coal

B - Rice

C - Fish

D - Grains and oilseed

The answer is D, Grains and oilseed

63) What is Saskatchewan rich in?

A - Grain

B - Uranium and potash

C - Manure

D - None of the above

The answer is B, Uranium and potash

64) What is Saskatchewan's largest city and the center of the mining industry?

A - Ottawa

B - Nunavut

C - Regina

D - Saskatoon

The answer is D, Saskatoon

65) Regina, the capital of Saskatchewan, is home to the training academy of which police force?

A - Uniformed Patrol Officers

B - Royal Canadian Mounted Police

C - Transit and railroad police

D - Municipal Police

The answer is B, Royal Canadian Mounted Police

66) What is the most populous Prairie province?

A - Saskatchewan

B - Alberta

C - Manitoba

D - Ontario

The answer is B, Alberta

67) Where did Alberta and Lake Louise get their names?

A - From Queen Victoria

B - From the Prime Minister

C - From the Aboriginals

D - Princess Louise Caroline Alberta

The answer is D, Princess Louise Caroline Alberta

68) How many national parks does Alberta have?

A - 5

B - 8

C - 6

D - 4

The answer is A, 5

69) When was Banff National Park established?

A - 1889

B - 1985

C - 1990

D - 1885

The answer is D, 1885

70) Alberta is the largest producer of what?

A - Grain

B - Coal

C - Oil and gas

D - Hydro-electric

The answer is C, Oil and gas

71) What is Alberta renowned for that makes Canada one of the world's major beef producers?

A - Large import of beefs

B - Vast cattle ranches

C - A lot of green pastures

D - None of the above

The answer is B, Vast cattle ranches

72) What is British Columbia known as?

A - Canada's Pacific gateway

B - British Columbia bridge

C - St. John's gateway

D - British Columbia gateway

The answer is A, Canada's Pacific gateway

73) What is Canada's largest and busiest port which also handles billions of dollars in goods traded around the world?

A - British Columbia port

B - West Coast port

C - Port of Vancouver

D - Pacific port

The answer C, Port of Vancouver

74) Which has the most expensive park system in Canada?

A - British Columbia

B - Ontario

C - Alberta

D - Vancouver

The answer is A, British Columbia

75) What is the approximate number of parks that British Columbia has?

A - Approximately 400 provincial parks

B - Approximately 500 provincial parks

C - Approximately 600 provincial parks

D - Approximately 700 provincial parks

The answer is C, approximately 600 provincial parks

76) What are the most spoken languages in British Columbia after English?

A - French and Punjabi

B - Chinese and Punjabi

C - Tagalog and Chinese

D - Chinese and Irish

The answer is B, Chinese and Punjabi

77) The capital city Victoria, is a tourist center and base of what fleet?

A - Marine's Pacific Fleet

B - Canada's Atlantic Fleet

C - Navy's Atlantic Fleet

D - Navy's Pacific Fleet

The answer is D, Navy's Pacific Fleet

78) These northwestern territories contain 1/3 of Canada's land mass - but only have a population of around 100,000 people.
A - Nunavut and Yukon
B - Nunavut and Northwest
C - Yukon and Ontario
D - Quebec and Nunavut

The answer is A, Nunavut and Yukon

79) What is the north often referred to as?
A - Land of the Midnight Sun
B - Land of the Morning Sun
C - Land of the North
D - Northern Star

The answer is A, Land of the midnight sun

80) In the height of summer, how long can the daylight last in the north?
A - 16 hours
B - 20 hours
C - 24 hours
D - 12 hours

The answer is C, 24 hours

81) In winter, how many months does the sun disappear and darkness sets in for?
A - 4 months
B - 3 months
C - 7 months

D - 10 months

The answer is B, 3 months

82) Large areas of the north are made up of what?
A - Frost
B - Forrest
C - Tundra
D - Pasture

The answer is C, Tundra

83) What do the people of the north commonly do to earn a living?
A - Fishing
B - Hunting
C - Farming
D - Trapping

The answer is C, Farming

84) Which of the following mines are found in the north?
A - Lead
B - Gold
C - Zinc
D - All of the above

The answer is D, All of the above

85) During what event did thousands of miners come to Yukon?
A - Silver Rush of the 1990s
B - Gold Rush of the 1890s
C - Diamond Rush of 1870s
D - Copper Rush of 1880s

The answer is B, Gold Rush of the 1890s

86) What opened from Skagway in neighboring Alaska to the territorial capital, Whitehorse, which provides a tourist expedition across risky passes and bridges?
A - White Pass and Yukon Railway
B - Alaska Pass and Yukon Train
C - Whitehorse Pass and Alaska Trail
D - Alaska Pass and Yukon Train

The answer is A, White Pass and Yukon Railway

87) In which year was the pass and railway opened?
A - 1700
B - 1600
C - 1800
D - 1900

The answer is D, 1900

88) Yukon holds the bragging rights for the coldest temperature on record in Canada, at what temperature?
A - (-83°C)

B - (-63°C)
C - (-53°C)
D - (-73°C)

The answer is B, (-63°C)

89) What is the highest mountain in Canada?
   A - Mount Canada
   B - Mount Everest
   C - Mount Yukon
   D - Mount Logan

The answer is D, Mount Logan

90) Who is the world-famous geologist in which the highest mountain in Canada was named after?
   A - Sir William Logan
   B - Sir Wilbert Logan
   C - Sir Wilson Logan
   D - Sir Wilfred Logan

The answer is A, Sir William Logan

91) What was formed from "Rupert's Land" and the North-Western Territory in 1870?
   A - Northeast Territories
   B - North-South Territories
   C - Northwest Territories (N.W.T)
   D - None of the Above

The answer is C, Northwest Territories (N.W.T)

92) What is the name of the capital that is called the diamond capital of North America?

A - Yellowstone

B - Yellowknife

C - Red Valley

D - Redstone

The answer is B, Yellowknife

93) What is the second-longest river in North America (after the Mississippi)?

A - Canada River

B - St. John's River

C - Mackenzie River

D - Nile River

The answer is D, Mackenzie River

94) What does Nunavut mean in Inuktitut?

A - Our land

B - Our community

C - Our farm

D - Our people

The answer is A, Our land

95) In what year was Nunavut established?

A - 1980

B - 1976

C - 1996

D - 1999

The answer is D, 1999

96) What is the capital of Nunavut?
A - Iqaluit
B - Yellowknife
C - Ontario
D - Regina

The answer is A, Iqaluit

97) What was the capital formerly known as?
A - Inuit Bay
B - Fortune Bay
C - Frobisher Bay
D - Fisher's Bay

The answer is C, Frobisher Bay

98) Who was the capital (Frobisher Bay) named after?
A - Mark Frobisher
B - Marco Frobisher
C - Marcel Frobisher
D - Martin Frobisher

The answer is D, Martin Frobisher

99) What is the official language of Nunavut and the first language in schools?
A - Michif
B - Inuktitut
C - Aboriginal
D - Metis

The answer is B, Inuktitut

100) How does the 19-member Legislative Assembly choose a premier and ministers?

A - By consensus

B - By debate

C - By hunting

D - From the Prime Minister's suggestion

The answer is A, By consensus

101)   Who deals with the harsh weather conditions in an isolated region to secure and keep the flag flying in Canada's Arctic?

A - Canadian Rangers

B - Royal Canadian Mounted Police

C - Governor-General

D - Mayor

The answer is A, Canadian Rangers

102)   Canadian Rangers are part of what police force?

A - Royal Canadian Mounted Police

B - Canada's National Police Force

C - Canadian Forces Reserves (militia)

D - Railway Police

The answer is C, Canadian Forces Reserves (militia)

103)   What do the Rangers use to travel during winter?

A - Sled

B - Ski

C - Snowmobile

D - Tram

The answer is C, Snowmobile

104)   What do you call the popular game for hunters, and a symbol of Canada's North?

A - Caribou

B - Hockey

C - Basketball

D - Skating

The answer is A, Caribou

105)   What is a Caribou?

A - Raccoon

B - Eagle

C - Beaver

D - Reindeer

The answer is D, Reindeer

True or False Answers

1) True or False, Canada is part of the United States.

The answer is False, Canada is not part of the USA.

2) True or False, Canadians cannot leave the country freely.

The answer is False, Canadians can leave the country freely.

3) True or False, Habeas Corpus is derived from French common law.

The answer is False, Habeas Corpus comes from English common law.

4) True or False, Aboriginal People have rights.

The answer is True.

5) True or False, mobility rights are a fundamental characteristic of Canadian heritage and identity.

The answer is False, these are not related to heritage.

6) **True or False, The Constitution of Canada was changed in 1982.**

The answer is True.

7) **True or False, the Prime Minister of Canada is above the law.**

The answer is False, no person or group is above the law.

8) **True or False, voting rights give citizens responsibility to vote in federal, provincial or territorial and local elections**

The answer is True.

9) **True or False, all citizens should protect Canada's natural, cultural, and architectural heritage for the future.**

The answer is True.

10) **True or False, joining the military service is forced in Canada.**

The answer is False, there is no compulsory military service in Canada.

11) **True or False, Canada is known for being a strong and free country.**

The answer is True.

12) True or False, Canada is the only Constitutional Monarch in the world.

The answer is False, Canada is the only Constitutional Monarch in North America.

13) True or False, Canada's original constitutional document was formed in 1864.

The answer is False, the original constitutional document was created in 1867.

14) True or False, many poets/songwriters have hailed Canada as the Great Land.

The answer is False, they instead called it the Great Dominion.

15) True or False, Canada has five founding groups.

The answer is False, Canada has three founding groups - aboriginal, British & French.

16) True or False, the ancestors of Aboriginal people are thought to have migrated from Australia.

The answer is False, they migrated from Asia.

17) True or False, territorial rights were first granted through the Royal Proclamation by Queen Elizabeth II.

The answer is False, they were granted in the Royal Proclamation by King George the 3rd.

18) True or False, the government put Aboriginal children in residential schools to incorporate them into Canadian culture, while Aboriginal practices were prohibited.

The answer is True.

19) True or False, the term Aboriginal peoples refers to three distinct groups: Indian, Inuit, and Métis/Inuit.

The answer is True.

20) True or False, Inuit means "the people" in the Michif language.

The answer is False, it means "the people" in Inuktitut language.

21) True or False, the Métis mostly live in the Prairies.

The answer is True.

22) True or False, roughly 65% of Aboriginal people are First Nations, while 30% are Métis, and 4% are Inuit.

The answer is True.

23) True or False, the Acadians are descendants of French colonists who began settling in Canada in 1604.

The answer is True.

24) True or False, the war where Arcadians were deported from their homeland is known as the Great Ordeal.

The answer is False, it is known as the Great Upheaval.

25) True or False, people who speak French as their first language are called Anglophones.

The answer is False, they are called Francophones.

26) True or False, English speakers are called Anglophones.

The answer is True.

27) True or False, the Prime Minister recognized that Quebecois formed a nation within united Canada.

The answer is False, The House of Commons recognized this about the Quebecois.

28) True or False, Canada's diversity does not include gay and lesbians.

The answer is False, Canada's diversity includes gay and lesbians, who can access civil marriage.

29) True or False, most Canadians identify as Christian.

The answer is True.

30) True or False, the first explorers of Canada thought they reached the East Indies.

The answer is True.

31) True or False, John Cabot was an English immigrant to Canada.

The answer is False, John Cabot was an Italian immigrant to England.

32) True or False, Jacques Cartier was the first European to find what we now call Québec City and Montreal.

The answer is True.

33) True or False, in the 1550s, the word Canada first appeared on maps.

The answer is True.

34) True or False, Pierre de Monts/Samuel de Champlain were Italian explorers.

The answer is False, they were French.

35) True or False, the fur-trade was driven by the need for raccoon pelts in Europe.

The answer is False, beaver pelts were required in Europe which sparked the fur trade.

36) True or False, The Quebec Act of 1774 allowed gender freedom.

The answer is False, it allows religious freedom.

37) True or False, The Quebec Act also restored French civil law while keeping British criminal law.

The answer is True.

38) **True or False, King Charles II granted the Hudson's Bay Company exclusive rights for watershed draining in 1770 - effectively creating a monopoly.**

The answer is False, that was in 1670.

39) **True or False, in 1759, the British overpowered the French in the "Battle of the Plains. "**

The answer is True.

40) **True or False, in 1792, black Nova Scotians established Scottown in Sierra Leone.**

The answer is False, it was called Freetown.

41) **True or False, The Constitutional Act of 1791 gave way for the name Canada to become official.**

The answer is True.

42) **True or False, the first companies in Canada were formed during competition over mining.**

The answer is False, the competition was related to the sale of fur.

43) True or False, The Provincial Freeman is a newspaper focused on women's rights.

The answer is False, the newspaper is dedicated to anti-slavery & black immigration, as well as reducing alcohol consumption.

44) True or False, Montreal's Stock Exchange opened officially in 1832.

The answer is True.

45) True or False, in 1814, Robert Ross led an event where the White house was set on fire and burned down.

The answer is True.

46) True or False, armed rebels were defeated by Irish troops and Canadian volunteers in 1837-38, outside of Montreal and Toronto.

The answer is False, the troops were British - not Irish.

47) True or False, Lord Durham said the best way for the Canadians to achieve progress was to take part in Muslim culture.

The answer is False, he said they should do it through Protestant culture.

48) True or False, Nova Scotia attained full responsible government in 1847-48.

The answer is True.

49) True or False, until 1982, July 1 was called "Dominion Day" - now, however, it is known as Canada Day.

The answer is True.

50) True or False, Prime Minister Trudeau established the North West Mounted Police force.

The answer is False, Prime Minister Macdonald established the NWMP.

51) True or False, British Columbia joined Canada when Ottawa promised to build a bridge to the West.

The answer is False, Ottawa instead promised to build a railway to the West Coast.

52) True or False, Ottawa formed the Canadian Expeditionary Force in 1914.

The answer is True.

53) True or False, Sir Arthur Currie was known as Canada's greatest soldier.

The answer is True.

54) True or False, Dr. Emily Stowe was the first Canadian lady to work professionally in medicine in Canada.

The answer is True.

55) True or False, Remembrance Day takes place on November 21st, every year.

The answer is False, It's on November 11th.

56) True or False, Canada's Central Bank was formed in 1934.

The answer is True.

57) True or False, Canadians captured Juno Beach in the 1st World War.

The answer is False, that was during the 2nd World War.

58) True or False, The Canadian Army helped free the Netherlands in 1945.

The answer is True.

59) True or False, The Royal Canadian Navy protected merchant ships from German submarines.

The answer is True.

60) **True or False, the cold war was initiated by the Soviet Union - under dictator Josef Stalin.**

The answer is True.

61) **True or False, the push for Quebec sovereignty was overpowered in 1930.**

The answer is False, this was in 1980.

62) **True or False, Dr. Wilfred Penfield was known as the greatest living Canadian.**

The answer is True.

63) **True or False, the federal government takes responsibility for matters like defense, currency, and citizenship.**

The answer is True.

64) **True or False, the Parliament has two distinct parts - the Sovereign and the House of Commons.**

The answer is False, the Parliament actually has three parts including the Sovereign, Senate and House of Commons.

65) True or False, the Prime Minister in office chooses the Cabinet ministers.

The answer is True.

66) True or False, the three northern territories (Yukon, Northwest Territories, and Nunavut) don't have the status of provinces.

The answer is True.

67) True or False, the Governor directs the governing of Canada.

The answer is False, The Prime Minister directs the governing of Canada.

68) True or False, in the three Northern territories, the mayor has a ceremonial role.

The answer is False, the Commissioner has a ceremonial role.

69) True or False, everyone in the electoral district can vote for the party of their choice.

The answer is True.

70) **True or False, the Prime Minister decides the Crown ministers.**

The answer is True.

71) **True or False, after an election, the PM is appointed by the Governor General.**

The answer is True.

72) **True or False, right now, there are three main parties - the Conservatives, New Democrats, and the Liberals.**

The answer is True.

73) **True or False, the Prime Minister and Cabinet ministers, together, are referred to as the shelf.**

The answer is False, they are called the Cabinet.

74) **True or False, the Voter Information Card confirms that you are on the list of voters and states who you voted for.**

The answer is False, the Voter Information Card does not show information on who you voted for.

75) True or False, provincial, territorial, and municipal elections have the same rules as federal elections.

The answer is False, the rules are different.

76) True or False, the First Nations have responsibilities including housing & schools.

The answer is True.

77) True or False, the legal system is formed upon the rule of law, democratic principles, and due process, amongst other things.

The answer is True.

78) True or False, freedom under the law is the principle where the government must respect a person's legal rights.

The answer is False, this is known as due process.

79) True or False, you can question the police about their service or conduct.
The answer is True.

80) True or False, the Crown has been the symbol of French royalty for more than 1,000 years.

The answer is False, instead it is the Fleur-de-Lys.

81) True or False, the beaver is Canada's best-known symbol.

The answer is False, the Maple leaf is Canada's most widely recognized symbol.

82) True or False, many young Canadians play hockey at school.

The answer is True.

83) True or False, The Royal Anthem of Canada (God Save the King) can be when Canadians want to honor the sovereign.

The answer is True.

84) True or False, November 30th is the day of Sir Wilfrid Laurier.

The answer is False, November 20th is the day of Sir Wilfrid Laurier.

85) True or False, today, Canada is part of the G8.

The answer is True.

86) True or False, greater than 75% of Canadians work in service-based industries.

The answer is True.

87) True or False, Ottawa is Canada's largest metropolitan area.

The answer is False, Ottawa is Canada's 4th largest metro area.

88) True or False, Nova Scotia has a history of hydro-electric dams.

The answer is False, Nova Scotia has a history of coal mining, forestry and other agriculture.

89) True or False, New Brunswick is <u>officially the only</u> bilingual province of Canada.

The answer is True.

90) True or False, Quebecers are leaders in industries such as pharmaceuticals and electronics.

The answer is False, they are leaders in industries like pharmaceuticals and aeronautics.

91) True or False, Manitoba is the center of Ukrainian life in Canada, with 14% of the population having Ukrainian origin.

The answer is True.

92) True or False, Alberta is the biggest producer of oil and gas (O&G) in Canada.

The answer is True.

THE CANADIAN CITIZENSHIP TEST

93) True or False, half of all the goods produced in British Columbia are dairy products.

The answer is False, half of the products are forestry related.

94) True or False, there are trees on the tundra.

The answer is False, there are no trees on the frozen soil.

95) True or False, Wilson Logan is one of Canada's greatest scientists.

The answer is False, he was called Sir William Logan.

96) True or False, more than 50% of the population in the Northwest Territories are Aboriginal.

The answer is True.

97) True or False, Michif is an official and the first school language in Nunavut.

The answer is False, Inuktitut is the first and official language in schools.

98) True or False, The Badlands of Ontario are home to prehistoric fossils and dinosaur relics.

The answer is False, the badlands are in Alberta.

99) True or False, Yukon's Capital is Whitehorse.

The answer is True.

100)   True or False, Canada is the third largest country on earth.

The answer is False, Canada is the second largest country.

BONUS: The Oath of Citizenship

"I swear (or affirm)
That I will be faithful
And bear true allegiance
To His Majesty
King Charles the Third
King of Canada
His Heirs and Successors
And that I will faithfully observe
The laws of Canada
Including the Constitution
Which recognizes and affirms
The Aboriginal and treaty rights of
First Nations, Inuit and Métis peoples
And fulfill my duties as a Canadian
citizen."

Conclusion

Thank you for buying and reading this book. We hope you found it useful in passing the Canadian Citizenship test.

If so, please leave us a 5* review on Amazon, it helps us more than you can imagine!

Best of luck and Welcome to Canada!

Yours, Toronto Publications

Manufactured by Amazon.ca
Bolton, ON